The Flight

The Flight

Confessions of an
Argentine Dirty Warrior

Horacio Verbitsky

Translated from
the Spanish by Esther Allen

The New Press
New York

Library of Congress Cataloging-in-Publication Data
Verbitsky, Horacio
[El vuelo. English]
The flight: confessions of an Argentinian dirty warrior / Horacio Verbitsky;
translated from the Spanish by Esther Allen.
p.   cm.
Includes bibliographical references.
ISBN 1-56584-009-7 (HC)
1. State-sponsored terrorism—Argentina. 2. Disappeared persons—Argentina.
3. Escuela de Mecánica de la Armada Argentina.
HV6433.A7V4713   1996
982.06'4'092—dc20
[B]   96-1032
CIP

Published in the United States by The New Press, New York
Distributed by W. W. Norton & Company, Inc., New York

Established in 1990 as a major alternative to the large, commercial publishing
houses, The New Press is a full-scale nonprofit American book publisher outside of
the university presses. The Press is operated editorially in the public interest, rather
than for private gain; it is committed to publishing in innovative ways works of
educational, cultural, and community value that, despite their intellectual merits,
might not normally be commercially viable. The New Press's editorial offices are
located at the City University of New York.

Book design by Ann Antoshak

Printed in the United States of America

9 8 7 6 5 4 3 2 1

To my sister Alicia

History is a nightmare from which I am trying to awake.

— James Joyce, *Ulysses*

Contents

Part I
Confession

Chapter One
Let's Tell the Truth

"I WAS at ESMA. I want to talk to you," he said when he came up to me in the Buenos Aires subway.

He was a short man with a big nose and a mustache, around forty-five, wearing blue pants and a striped, short-sleeved shirt, carrying a cheap portfolio. He looked like many of the survivors of the military dictatorship's most notorious secret concentration camp, who scramble to earn a living without ever freeing themselves from the bad dream. I thought he was one of them and told him I understood what he had been through.

"No, you don't understand. I'm one of Rolón's colleagues," he explained. In other words, not victim but victimizer.

Lieutenant Commander Juan Carlos Rolón was one of the officers in the intelligence unit at the Navy School of Mechanics (best known by its Spanish acronym, ESMA), where noncommissioned officers are trained in technical specialties. Rolón and his comrade-in-arms Antonio Pernías were at the heart of one of the major political crises of 1994. Carlos Menem, Argentina's president, decided to promote them both to the rank of captain (in the Argentine navy, the rank immediately below rear admiral). However, on the day the senate was to confirm their new rank, I came out with an account of their backgrounds in the Buenos Aires newspaper *Página/12*, where I publish a political column. I had been studying them for eighteen years, since 1976, when I wrote the first history of Argentina's dirty war.

In the 1980s, there were a number of important trials for human rights violations committed during the military regime of 1976 to 1983. A federal court of appeals arrested Pernías in 1987 on the charge of having tortured eleven prisoners, most of them women. The case had tremendous repercussions because the prisoners in question were the initial nucleus of the Mothers of the Plaza de Mayo, who were abducted from inside the Church of the Holy Cross on Christmas Eve 1977. Another navy officer, Alfredo Astiz, had infiltrated the group, pretending to be the brother of a disappeared person, and gave the signal for the abduction to begin by kissing one of the women. Among the group were two French nuns Alice Domon and Leonie Duquet. After being tortured, all of them were killed. The French court of appeals in Paris sentenced Astiz to life imprisonment, making him the only member of the Argentine military who cannot leave Argentina, even to wage war, without being arrested by the police.

Pernías was also accused of the murder of a group of priests in St. Patrick's Church, another of the most bloodcurdling cases of the 1970s. Rolón was investigated for the abduction of a woman who died resisting police who were trying to take her from her home. He was also head of the ESMA intelligence unit that attempted to brainwash a group of prisoners so that, under the threat of death, they would work to further the political career of Admiral Emilio Massera, a member of the military junta who wished to become a charismatic leader like former president Juan De Peron.

Argentina's president at the time, Raúl Alfonsín, in response to the uprising of an army group opposed to the prosecutions, passed two laws that saved Rolón and Pernías from jail. The law known as Full Stop (*Punto Final*) kept Rolón's case from coming to trial by making it impossible to prosecute cases that were not brought to the courts by a certain date. After half a year in jail, Pernías was set free by another law, Due Obedience (*Obediencia Debida*), which stated that officers of a certain rank and below were to be presumed by law to have been ignorant of the illegality of the orders they carried out.

In the meantime, the National Commission on the Disappeared, appointed by the president at the end of the dictatorship and made up of a dozen people from scientific, cultural, religious, and political spheres, had registered other accusations against the two. In Venezuela, Pernías and Rolón had attempted to kidnap the industrial tycoon Julio Broner. Pernías was planning to shoot darts coated with a drug that would paralyze Broner. In order to determine the exact dosage, he tested his darts on a prisoner who never reappeared alive. Pernías was also an instructor of a course on "antisubversive fighting" for torturers from Uruguay, Paraguay, Bolivia, Nicaragua, Brazil, and Guatemala. He started a real estate agency to sell property robbed from prisoners whose families were blackmailed into signing it over. Once the apartments were sold, the prisoners were killed.

Up to this point, the cases against Pernías and Rolón resembled a long succession of cases involving military promotions, going back to the end of the dictatorship. The press scrutinized the past behavior of the nominees and human rights organizations made their objections known to the Senate, which was simultaneously pressured to confirm the promotions by the government and the chiefs of staff of the three branches of the military. But this time something was different. Pernías and Rolón felt the navy had abandoned them; they decided to talk and unleashed a chain reaction. Until then, the military had denied the facts of the dirty war, discrediting witnesses by accusing them of continuing their political battle against the armed forces by other means.

Pernías broke with tradition by acknowledging that torture was the weapon of choice in a lawless war, admitting that the navy had participated in the abduction and murder of the French nuns, and suggesting that the priests in St. Patrick's had been killed by the federal police. Rolón's statement was less direct. He said that he would never under any circumstances give orders like the ones he had obeyed and that they "were wrong," but were handed down by "commanding officers who are now admirals, with the Senate's confirmation." He also let it be known that no one in the military had been able to keep his hands clean, because the navy had rotated all officers through the different task forces.

"Don't you think Rolón is getting shafted?" the man with the cheap portfolio asked.

"*What do you mean?*"

"Or do you think Rolón acted on his own initiative and we were some sort of rogue gang?"

"*What were you, if not a gang?*"

"Can a gang make use of naval installations, mobilize airplanes?"

"*Airplanes?*" So went this odd dialogue of questions and questions.

He opened the portfolio and took out a sheet of paper. "Read this. It will interest you."

It was a notarized letter addressed to the chief of staff of the navy, Admiral Enrique Emilio Molina Pico. If the members of the Senate Confirmation Committee denied Pernías and Rolón their promotions, it said, they would, out of ignorance, be committing an injustice. For that reason the navy should inform the public of "the methods those in the highest ranks ordered used at the Navy School of Mechanics for arresting, interrogating, and eliminating the enemy during the war against subversion and, if it exists, should publish the list of those inaccurately called the 'disappeared' (*desaparecidos*)."

"*Eliminating the enemy?*"

"Finish reading it."

"While stationed at ESMA, I carried out orders from commanding officers who are now admirals, with the confirmation of the Honorable Senate of the Nation." This phrase caught my attention. It was an indirect way of saying: all of us or none of us.

"*Those are the very words Rolón used.*"

"Keep reading."

"I hereby inform you that should the aforementioned confirmations be denied, I will demand a full judicial inquiry so that the truth can triumph over hypocrisy once and for all." The letter was signed by Lieutenant Commander Adolfo Francisco Scilingo, the man with the cheap portfolio.

"I have here an acknowledgment of receipt signed by Videla's guard," he added.

When Menem pardoned the former military leaders in 1990 and former military President Jorge Rafael Videla demanded a full vindication as well, Scilingo took another letter to Videla's house in person. This time the letter detailed the kinds of truth Scilingo intended to reveal if his demands were not met.

"Read it, but don't worry about remembering the details. I'll give you a copy. You'll see that we did worse things than the Nazis."

Scilingo's text is chilling:

> In 1977, as a lieutenant stationed at the Navy School of Mechanics (ESMA) with operative dependence on the First Corps of the army, when you were the commander-in-chief and in fulfillment of orders given by the Executive Power whose powers you then exercised, I participated in two aerial transports, the first with thirteen subversives aboard a Skyvan belonging to the coast guard, and the second with seventeen terrorists aboard an Electra belonging to naval aviation. The prisoners were told they were being taken to a prison in the

south and for that reason had to receive a vaccination. They
received an initial dose of anesthetic, which was reinforced by
another larger dose during the flight. Finally, in both cases,
they were stripped naked and thrown into the waters of the
South Atlantic from the planes during the flight. Personally, I
have never been able to overcome the shock that the execution
of that order caused me; despite the fact that we were in the
middle of the dirty war, this method of executing the enemy
doesn't seem to me to be a very ethical one for military men to
employ, but I believed that I would find in you the timely public acknowledgment of your responsibility for these facts.

In response to the matter of the disappeared, you said that
there are subversives living under assumed names, others who
died and were buried as persons unknown, and, finally, you
did not reject the possibility that certain excesses might have
been committed by your subordinates. Where do I fit into that?
Do you believe that the weekly transports were the result of
unauthorized excesses? Let's put an end to the cynicism. Let's
tell the truth. Let the list of the dead be known, even though at
the time of their deaths you did not assume responsibility for
having signed an order for their execution. The unjust sentence
you say you carried out bore the signature of the president
who ordered the trial, the signature of the prosecutor who
sought the conviction, the signature of the judges who established the sentence. Whether or not their action was mistaken,
all of them signed. We still bear the responsibility for thousands of disappeared persons without facing the facts or
speaking the truth, and you talk about vindication. Vindication is not achieved by decree.

It ends by announcing to Videla that if he does not assume his
responsibility, he, Scilingo, will publish the letter, "so that the
truth can be known."

"*What was Videla's answer?*"

"He never answered me."

Scilingo had then sent a copy of this letter to Admiral Jorge
Osvaldo Ferrer, whom President Menem has appointed as chief of
staff of the navy. In it Scilingo argued that by accepting the pardon, the former military leaders had acknowledged that
the verdict and life sentence given to Videla and Massera were not

politically motivated, as they had maintained during their trial. Therefore, their former subordinates "became the executors of orders that could be of a criminal nature." The Full Stop law freed them from any possibility of conviction, but "we are nevertheless responsible for the events in which we were participants," he wrote. He did not want to become responsible for a coverup "by not assuming the agency I had in cases of disappeared persons," and had resolved to present himself at the office of a federal prosecutor to make a declaration "so that it can be determined whether in the fulfillment of orders I have committed any illegal act."

As an officer of greater seniority than Commander Alfredo Aztiz, he also wished to make a declaration to the French judicial authorities "in order to explain the truth of the charges and achieve their just dismissal." Ferrer should order "the publication of the names of the subversives executed by members of the military, independently of the method that was used." Scilingo requested that his letter be brought to Menem's attention.

The sheaf of photocopies he took out of the portfolio included a second letter to Ferrer. Having received no response to the first one, he felt that he was not being led by his superiors but was being "used and cast aside." The Naval Military School "educated me to be a naval officer," but at the School of Mechanics "I was ordered to act outside of the law and transformed into a criminal." The attitude of his former superiors toward the amnesty "makes me an accomplice to a cover-up," he wrote.

The letter ended with a cryptic reference. He said that in civilian life he had made some serious mistakes "both in my personal conduct and at the corporate-financial level." He attributed them to the "pride, omnipotence, and excessive self-esteem I felt in dealing with civilians," acquired during the military dictatorship, "when I believed that both my commanding officers and myself were the saviors of the fatherland. The blows I have suffered have shown me that only truth, democracy, and justice are the true solution for our country."

He left a set of copies of these letters at the Military House of the Presidency, addressed to Menem. He asked for authorization to make a declaration to an Argentine federal prosecutor and to the French judicial authorities and to make his letter to Videla public. He also sought a private audience in which "to learn the thoughts of my commander in chief on the subject in question."

Menem never responded either.

Chapter Two
In Praise of Torture

MENEM DID not know who Pernías and Rolón were. Their names were included in the list of those nominated for promotions by his administration's secretary of military affairs, Vicente Massot, an ultrarightist Catholic intellectual who had written essays justifying Hitler and Franco. He had been a good friend of Admiral Rubén Jacinto Chamorro, the commander of the concentration camp where Pernías, Rolón, Astiz, and Scilingo carried out their orders. Massot, who used to visit Chamorro at ESMA, was the first civil servant in the constitutional government to defend torture publicly: "What we must ask ourselves, in Machiavellian terms, is up to what point, on certain occasions, does the end justify the means. A prisoner knows the location of a bomb about to explode that will kill hundreds of people. You could end up responsible for a bombing in an elementary school, for the death of hundreds of kids, because you refused to use torture," he said to justify the promotions.

The same riddle had been posed by General Albano Harguindeguy, minister of the interior under the dictatorship, to Miguel
Hesayne, bishop of Patagonia. "No, General. The end does not
justify the means," the austere priest answered. Hesayne pre-
dicted that "a victory at the cost of ignoble acts will quickly turn
into a defeat because an armed force that practices torture will
not escape unpunished by God the creator." He objected to the
choice "of Machiavellian principles, rejecting those of Christ
and his gospel" and said that "torture is immoral, regardless of
who employs it."

In any case, the Machiavellian conjecture offered by Massot
and Harguindeguy was based on false premises. Never did any
Argentine guerrilla organization attack an elementary school.
In the torture chambers, the prisoners were not interrogated
about bombs set to go off, but about their next appointment
with their comrades.

Menem frantically denied that he was attempting to reward
the executioner of the French nuns. "That is a clumsy lie. At no
time has the government favored promotions of that nature.
There is no possibility of that." The officers who had participated in tortures would not be promoted, he promised.

His answer caused some consternation in the government and
the navy. When told he had in fact signed the documents recom-
mending the promotions, Menem was hostage to his own
words. The Senate Confirmation Committee recommended that
the promotions be rejected. Their opinion was about to be rati-
fied in an open session, but the Government House called the
leader of the bloc controlled by the powerful Justicialista Party,
who requested that the committee reexamine the case.

It was agreed that Pernías and Rolón would appear in their
own defense before the Senate Confirmation Committee. If their
former commanders had been pardoned, those who had a much
lesser responsibility should be promoted, opined the chairman
of the committee, a Peronist senator who was his party's

defeated candidate for the vice presidency in 1983. Just when the seas started getting rough, however, the navy's top brass jumped ship: both the chief of staff, Molina Pico, and the assistant chief found reasons to be out of the country. Pernías and Rolón arrived at the Senate alone, wearing civilian clothing. Despite the fact that the Senate had not confirmed their promotions, they were already carrying out the duties of full captains. To exhibit their insignia in front of the senators would have been a provocation, and to disguise themselves in the uniforms of commanders would have diminished their authority in the eyes of their subordinates. The astonished senators, who did not even pressure them with questions, heard them acknowledge what the armed forces had been denying for almost two decades.

There was only one precedent. Retired Rear Admiral Horacio Mayorga had said in an article in 1985: "People are frightened and amazed by the Astiz affair. Do you know how many men like Astiz there were in the navy? Three hundred Astizes." The officers at ESMA were stern individuals who killed for the fatherland, "guys who never had a dime to their name. Astiz was a guy who had to go to the aircraft carrier to get a meal when his paycheck ran out. They were men who bet everything on what they were doing. Did they kill people? Of course. Everyone knows we eliminated them. Four or five were arrested, and how many of them were recuperable? One. And that was already a lot. The worst thing is what those men have to go through now. Many of them were thrown out of their houses by their wives, others lost their bearings completely, went crazy."

The speaker was not without a history. In 1972, Mayorga was the chief of the naval base in the southern city of Trelew, where one of the initial massacres, of two dozen political prisoners, was carried out on the pretext that they had attempted to escape. A decade later he offered to defend his two most notorious disciples, Chamorro and Astiz, before the military courts. Mayorga denied that at ESMA prisoners' fingers had been cut

off with a saw so they could not be identified by their finger-
prints. "That's a lie! The only thing we had at ESMA was the
electric cattle prod."

He also disagreed with the navy's conduct during that period.
"In my opinion, they should have put the prisoners in front of
firing squads in a soccer stadium, offered free Coca-Cola, and
broadcast the whole thing on television. I did not agree with the
way they were working in the shadows."

Mayorga tried to convince the United States writer Tina
Rosenberg of the navy's humanitarianism: "You should be asking me why we wasted an injection on those prisoners. But we
did." He said that he had seen terrible but unavoidable things
done in order to win the war, and he compared the men of the
navy with the members of the Uruguayan rugby team whose
plane had crashed high in the Andes a decade earlier and who,
in order to survive, had eaten the remains of their teammates
who died in the crash. Nevertheless, "They weren't cannibals,"
Mayorga said.

The rear admiral presented himself as a good Christian who
was troubled by his conscience. "We must condemn torture. The
day we stop condemning torture—although we tortured—the
day we become insensitive to mothers who lose their guerrilla
sons—although they are guerillas—is the day we stop being
human beings." But he denied that the gentlemen of the sea had
raped or stolen. "People talk about us as if we are savages. . . .
We are naval officials! We are not going to soil ourselves for
a gold watch!"

This initial and lone exception to the pact of silence had
no consequences. Mayorga had taken his retirement three years
earlier and his statements had been made to a little-known
magazine and to a writer who published them in a book only
years later.

Pernías and Rolón, however, remained on active duty and
were speaking in the first person as men who had personally

committed atrocities; the forum they chose was the national Senate, in front of journalists from all the media. The repercussions were immediate. The lawyer representing the families of the murdered nuns asked the committee to request precise information from Pernías as to where their remains were left, "in order to give them a Christian burial." Alain Juppé, the French minister of foreign affairs at that time, flew to Buenos Aires, met with the Argentine government as well as the Mothers of the Plaza de Mayo, and declared that, "when two French citizens are tortured and murdered for their way of thinking, France does not forget."

The murdered women had not belonged to a militaristic organization or even a political one; they were barely a dozen unarmed people whose only link was their kinship to others who had disappeared. At the moment the sacrilege took place, they were not setting off a bomb but collecting money in a church to publish a newspaper notice with a partial list of the disappeared.

Menem spent the first week of the crisis out of the country. His comments upon his return gave rise to as much astonishment as the revelations of the newly extroverted torturers: "There was a dirty war, and of the two parties involved in it, one was fighting for the rule of law and the others were constantly violating that law. I believe that the law triumphed on that occasion and we must keep that triumph intact." Pernías had just said that torture was the only law, and Menem chose to interpret this to mean that the law had triumphed.

The bloc of senators from the Justicialista Party decided not to consent to the promotions, but Menem only strengthened his support. At the army's headquarters he said, "Thanks to the presence of the armed forces, we triumphed in the dirty war." In front of the police force, he delivered an homage to Alberto Villar, the man who had organized the death squads that were active during the brief government of Isabelita Perón. And, during one of his daily radio broadcasts, he said that "above and beyond the mistakes that were made, the subversive apparatus disappeared, and we owe that to the men of the armed forces."

Menem's vehement defense of their shadowy past astounded the armed forces themselves. That same week, the chief of staff of the army, Lieutenant General Martín Balza, had said, "Nothing can be done about the past. We can only work on the present and the future. We must study the past very carefully, in a spirit of self-criticism and humility." Balza was the first chief of staff to express his loathing of the sinister logic that prevailed during the 1970s. "Ethics must always prevail. The end does not justify the means. There is no ethical justification of the ends when the procedures are illegitimate," he proclaimed. By requesting that the two commanders be promoted, the naval leadership and the executive branch were obstructing the transition of the military institutions from the swamp of the terrorist state to a modern role, compatible with democratic order.

Not even Menem's attempts to intervene lessened the impact of Pernías and Rolón's pronouncements on the navy. With these two fundamental bricks removed, the whole wall of silence could collapse. Scilingo went to the post office and mailed his notarized letter to Molina Pico. If the navy was not going to tell the truth, this time he would.

Chapter Three
A Christian Death

AT OUR first two meetings, Scilingo had told me his story. At the third, he was to document it. He arrived precisely at the time we had agreed upon. He hadn't changed his mind. He brought along the photocopies of the letters he had promised me.

"Now you can be certain I'm not going to back away from this," he said.

The only thing left was record his voice.

"Wait, don't start the tape," he resisted. "We have to prepare a list of questions today."

"*No, we're going to record this.*"

The tape began to turn. He reached out to stop it.

"*Leave the tape recorder alone.*"

Scilingo withdrew his hand. It was his turn to answer. He began the confession he had postponed for eighteen years.

"*How did the orders to throw defenseless prisoners into the ocean come to you?*"

"The first information I got about it was in 1976 from Admiral Luis María Mandía, who was the chief of naval operations, in front of the top ranking officers of all the units in the area of Puerto Belgrano (the Argentine Navy's largest base). He stated that special military operations that would employ means appropriate to the circumstances were being planned in order to meet the demands of a fight against an unforeseen enemy in which standard operating procedures would prove inapplicable. Ever since the Colonial era, he explained, uniforms had been used to differentiate between the two factions in a conflict. Later, they served as camouflage on different types of terrain. Now we would use civilian clothing as camouflage within the civilian sphere. All the officers in the Puerto Belgrano region were there, in the base's movie theater. Regarding the subversives who were condemned to death or who were to be eliminated, he commented that they were going to fly, and since there were people who have problems, some of them were not going to reach their destination. And he said that the Church authorities, at what level I don't know, had been consulted to try and find a way that was Christian and not too violent."

"*Who sentenced them and how were they sentenced?*"

"At ESMA, Admiral Chamorro was always number one. I don't know if he consulted any other authority or if the decision came from him. For me, it wasn't worth discussing. I imagine it was fully evaluated. We were convinced it was the most humanitarian thing to do, as Mendía said."

"*Did anyone ask Mendía any questions?*"

"Yes."

"*What did they ask him?*"

"I don't remember. I think one of the questions was about the uniforms. That was something unexpected. Since it wasn't a naval meeting, it had an impact."

"*Did Mendía present this as a decision that had been made?*"

"It appeared in the navy's written plans: special military operations. That was what he explained, what was planned there in terms of the institution's operating structures. The 3.3 Task Force, which operated at the Navy School of Mechanics, was provided for there.

"A military order must be clear and precise. From what you are saying, Mendía transmitted a nebulous concept with an elliptical phrase."

"It was a general description of the matter. He presented an overview of the situation. He didn't give any details since that was done afterward in each unit."

"You say it appeared in writing. But the flights do not appear in the naval plans that were made public later, during the 1985 trial."

"No. What appeared in writing was "'special military operations.'"

"Specifically, how did the transports you mention in your letter to Videla take place?"

"The ones I participated in?"

"Yes. How did you receive the orders?"

"My immediate superior officer gave them to me. In mid-1977, while I was stationed at the Navy School of Mechanics, I was called in by the head of defense, Commander Adolfo Mario Arduino. He was third in command, but he acted as second after Captain Salvio Menéndez was wounded. Arduino informs me that I have to make a flight, that I have to present myself in Dorado, which was the command center where orders were given. It operated in the officers' building. It was totally logical at that time, given that it was a rotating duty, and could be given to anyone—the whole navy was involved. It was an order and it was carried out. There was no doubt about it. It wasn't something unusual or hidden. Arduino later became a vice admiral and chief of naval operations."

"Nevertheless, in the task forces themselves, rank was not respected; the chain of command was broken."

"They were commando groups. Afterward everything went back to normal, to the level of authority that corresponded to each one. They were secret operations."

"No one ever paid much attention to the fact that a decision as serious as killing people did not come down by the normal procedure, approved and countersigned in a responsible fashion?"

"No. There isn't an armed force in the world where all orders are delivered in writing; it would be impossible to command. The system that was established to eliminate the subversive elements was institutionally based. It could order execution by firing squad as easily as any other type of elimination. As you can imagine, airplanes are not deployed by a gang, but by an armed force. The orders we were receiving were extreme, but they made sense in the context of the war that was being fought—both those to arrest the enemy and those to eliminate the enemy."

"No one ever asked why you weren't given signed orders for a shooting to be carried out publicly, by firing squad?"

"Yes, it was one of the things that was brought up in the meeting with the chief of naval operations. What happened to the prisoners was not made known, in order to withhold information from the enemy and create uncertainty. That was the theoretical reason we were given. Time would prove that the real reason was something else, because many years later, during the trials, no one said what had happened."

"You think that at that point they were already thinking about how to evade responsibility?"

"At that point, I don't know. But they did evade responsibility later, I have no doubt about that. Why, up to this very moment, hasn't the truth been made public, after twenty years? If the orders were all legal, what are they hiding? Why doesn't Congress have all the facts in hand in order to decide whether to promote Rolón or Pernías or, soon, Astiz?"

"*What happens when you show up at Dorado?*"

"There's an order on a blackboard indicating who will make up the convoy that is to go to the Buenos Aires military airport with the prisoners."

"*Did it say 'convoy that is to go to the airport'?*"

"I don't remember the exact words, but it was the convoy that was going to the airport.

"*In conversations among yourselves, how did you refer to this?*"

"The flight."

"*The flight?*"

"It was called a flight. It was normal, although now it seems like an aberration. Pernías and Rolón told the senators that the use of torture for extracting information from the enemy had been adopted as a standard practice, and this was too. Within that framework, caught up in the war we were convinced we were waging, it was one of the methodologies."

"*On the blackboard you saw your name and those of the others who were to go?*"

"The assumed name."

"*You didn't know each other's real names?*"

"Yes, everyone knew. In the navy we all know each other."

"*What was the point of using the cover names?*"

"So the enemy wouldn't find out who we were. Within the school there were subversives who were collaborating with us. In fact, when someone came in wearing a uniform, he was generally ordered to take his insignia off the collar so his rank couldn't be identified."

"*Describe the next step to me.*"

"I went to the basement, where the ones who were going to fly were. There was no one left lower down. They were informed that they were going to be transferred to the south and would be given a vaccination for that reason. They were given a vaccination—I mean a dose of something to knock them out, a sedative.

It made them drowsy."

"*A dose of what?*"

"I don't know. An injection."

"*Who administered it?*"

"One of the doctors stationed there."

"*A navy doctor?*"

"Yes. Then they were put on a navy truck, a green truck with a canopy. We went to the military airport, we entered from the back, and there we learned that it wasn't a navy Electra but a Skyvan belonging to the coast guard which was going to make the flight. Since we couldn't all fit on board, we divided the group that was going to fly, in half. I was only along as an errand boy. I don't know why they put me in charge of the first flight. Two of us got on the plane: me and the man who was my boss and supervisor in the automobile shop, Lieutenant Vaca, who later turned out not to be a Lieutenant Vaca at all, but a civilian lawyer who had been hired, a cousin of (the task force's chief of intelligence) Tigre Acosta. Then the subversives were carried out like zombies and loaded onto the airplane."

"*Do you continue to think of them as 'subversives' or are you using the term now because we are recording this?*"

"I'm describing the facts as they were at that moment."

"*That's why I changed the tense. Do you still think of them as subversives now?*"

"No."

"*How would you describe them today?*"

"Today, unfortunately, as things have played out, and since the military leaders keep hiding everything and not showing their faces, I think that both those who died in that way, because they were risking their lives, and we who were there, were two groups of useful idiots. I think they were using us. How many important subversives died? Who were the ones who died?"

"*Who were they?*"

"I don't think anyone died who had any tremendous impor-

tance that could have affected. . . . Yes, the country was in a
chaotic situation. But I'm telling you, today I think the problem
could have been solved another way. That's what I think today,
and there was no need to kill them. They could have been hidden
anywhere in the country. The armed forces weren't the only ones
responsible. A large part of the country consented to the barbar-
ities that were being committed."

"How was that consent expressed?"

"I don't think society acted out of terror. I think that it
appealed to the armed forces or that it backed what they did.
A certain excessiveness in the procedures, as it was called at
the time, was not rejected. It was accepted. Very few voices
were raised against it. If the majority of the population had
demonstrated against it, things would have been different.
Today I'm telling you that it was a barbaric thing. At that time
we were totally convinced of what we were doing. The way we
had internalized it, with the situation we were living through in
this country, it would be a total lie if I told you that I wouldn't do
it again under the same conditions. I would be a hypocrite.
When I did what I did I was convinced they were subversives.
What happens is that, as I tell you about this right now—and
I'm telling you about it in detail, since you ask me to and I
believe the truth must be known—don't think that it makes me
very happy or that it makes me feel very good. Right now I can't
say that they were subversives. They were human beings. We
were so deeply convinced that no one questioned it. There was
no other option, as Rolón said in the Senate. Most of the men
participated in a flight. It was done in order to rotate people, a
kind of communion."

"What did that communion consist of?"

"It was something that you had to do. I don't know what executioners go through when they have to kill, to drop the blade or
pull the switch on the electric chair. No one liked to do it, it wasn't
a pleasant thing. But it was done, and it was understood that this

was the best way. It wasn't discussed. It was something supreme that was done for the sake of the country. A supreme act. It's very difficult to understand and to explain, especially after so much time has gone by and I'm seeing things differently.

"The word "communion" has a mystical, charismatic component."

"Yes, that's how it was. When the order was received, it wasn't spoken of again. It was carried out automatically."

"Everyone participated?"

"They were rotated through from all over the country. A few may have stayed out of it, but only by chance. If it had been a small group—but it wasn't, it was the whole navy. ESMA had its permanent staff, the task force, which was assigned there indefinitely, and another temporary group that stayed for three months. Moreover, officers from across the country were sent to ESMA on assignment, for a weekend or a day. The flights were on Wednesdays. The staff went out and executed legal orders, and they didn't kill or murder. They captured and handed over. The brainwashing was total. The people who were picked up were interrogated in half an hour—there wasn't any more time than that—and then Chamorro decided who was going to die."

"What was the prisoners' reaction when they were told about the vaccination and the transfer?"

"They were glad."

"They didn't suspect what was going on?"

"Not at all."

"How long did it take for the drug to make them drowsy?"

"A short time."

"During the trip?"

"No, before leaving."

"The truck went as part of a convoy—"

"—with other vehicles acting as an escort. The prisoners were like zombies."

"But they could move in order to board the plane."

"This line of questioning is somewhat gruesome, totally gruesome. It's a fact, real and concrete. If you want me to describe it to you, I'll describe it to you."

"It's unavoidable. You mention it in the letter to Videla."

"Because it's the truth, it's what happened. Or do you have some doubt about that?"

"None whatsoever. Could they walk onto the airplane despite the drug?"

"No. They had to be helped."

"They were not aware of what was happening?"

"I have no doubt about that. No one was aware he was going to die."

"The fact that they had received what they thought was a vaccination and they could feel that they were becoming like zombies didn't make them . . ."

"No, no, no."

"The flight takes off. What happens then?"

"I don't feel like going on."

This time he succeeded in turning off the tape recorder.

"Why don't you want to go on?"

"Because I don't. Next time."

With the tape recorder off, he relaxes. He grows animated again when his favorite subject is brought up and he agrees to continue recording.

"You said that if Pernías, Rolón and Astiz cannot be promoted, then those with greater seniority should not have been promoted either."

"As far as I'm concerned, from Admiral Massera down to the most recent one, who I think was Astiz, no one could have stayed in the navy. It was all by rotation. Everyone in the navy knew, and in some cases a few men, who we thought were traitors, left. It was unavoidable. It was not spoken of. We were all convinced it was the best thing that could be done for the country, and furthermore these were military orders. Now look at the results."

"Yes."

"Not the results of the murders that were committed, but of all those who didn't speak. I'm not saying that Arduino shouldn't have been made a vice admiral, because I am no one to pass judgment on him. But if *he* can be, then Rolón can be. The chief of staff, Admiral Molina Pico, I don't know why he's afraid and hides it. It must be because everything we did was outside the law. In that case we're criminals and they all have to go. That's the issue. That's what I think.

"What was Molina Pico's participation during that period?"

"I don't know. But he must have had something to do with it. At the very least he was in the navy. He wasn't twittering around in a cloud of little birds."

"In the Navy School of Mechanics, were there any crews that did not rotate?"

"There was a permanent group in Dorado and a group that rotated every three months, that came from different navy posts."

"Was it only the permanent group in Dorado that participated in the flights?"

"No, no. It was completely a rotating duty. It was the whole navy, it wasn't a gang."

"Including those who were permanently stationed at the school?"

"Yes."

"Those who came for three months also participated?"

"Not only did those who were there for three months participate, but also others who were stationed elsewhere and who were sent to take part in flights, specifically. In other words, to involve them in it. The whole navy was involved in the fight against the subversives, or in the—now I don't know what it was. Because if it was an institutional fight against subversion, I don't know what there is to hide."

"You keep repeating that you weren't a gang."

"If you believe that a gang of ten guys can succeed in mobilizing airplanes belonging to the coast guard and the navy, you're a little bit mistaken. It was an armed force that was mobilizing. The big difference between us is that you call it a gang. I say that the navy acted as the navy, until I started having doubts. Why isn't the truth being told, if we were acting as the Argentine Navy, if we were carrying out orders handed down in perfectly correct fashion through the chain of command? The whole navy knew what was being done."

"The Sicilian Mafia obeyed the orders of Totó Riina. Obeying orders alone is not the qualifying characteristic of an institution."

"But if you are part of an armed organization, you're always receiving orders, carrying out orders, and giving orders. In the navy there are no comrades, there are men with greater and lesser seniority."

"But those orders must be legal."

"These were legal orders. In the navy there's no such thing as orders that aren't legal. Now if you ask me what I think today, it's different—but at that time I had no doubt."

"What do you think today?"

"If they had been legal orders, no one would be ashamed of telling everyone what happened, how the fight was carried on. However, this strange concealment or cover-up, this mystery. . . Someone said something about a blood pact, but there was no pact. No one ever told me I couldn't talk about it. How could I accept it if someone were to tell me I couldn't talk about it? It's acceptable not to speak, because these are wartime secrets, for a given period of time. But once the war is over, this belongs to history, and I even think it does the republic good to know what was done—and also it is imperative that the lists of those brought down or killed be given out, by whatever system, so that once and for all we can be done with this bizarre situation of disappeared people."

"Who has those lists?"

"I don't know who has them right now. But within the institutional framework, not at the level of a gang, the information came down through the command that, in one of the last meetings of the military junta, then-admiral Massera, before leaving, had stated that it was indispensable to make known the list of the disappeared. According to what we were told through the chain of command, the other members of the junta, and Videla especially, rejected this idea."

"As you understand it, do such lists exist?"

"They have to exist. At that time they existed. I believe that the chiefs of staff must have them. That is the logical thing. Lists of the dead can't be thrown out, if it's true that the military leadership acted as I had believed they did. Now if, as I suspect, they acted in a strange, odd and shadowy way, because now we aren't telling the truth . . . I don't know. . . . It may be that some chief of staff has thrown them out. It would be interesting if that were made public. I brought this up in some of my letters, but never got an answer.

"You insist that they were not a gang. But in one of your letters you say that in the Navy School of Mechanics you were ordered to act outside the law and were made into a criminal."

"Yes. You are asking me what we did. And I was totally convinced. When Alfonsín takes power, the juntas are put on trial. They say it's a political problem. They are found guilty and sentenced. They insist that it is a political problem. But afterward they are pardoned and they accept that without a problem. So what happened with everything that went on before? If the pardon is accepted, that means that the sentence is accepted, along with everything that happened before, the trial. It means that everything is true and none of it was a political game. It means that they were acting outside the law."

"But you didn't need them to accept the pardon in order to know that they were acting outside the law and that the statements made during the trial were true. The survivors talked

about exactly the same thing you lived through. All the stories of the victims and the human rights organizations that were heard during the trial coincide with your story."

"Did Videla say that?"

"No."

"And why didn't he say it?"

"Why do you think he didn't say it?"

"It's hard for me to accept it. If you ask me to define for you whether we were acting within or outside of the law, I believe we were acting like common criminals. It's very hard for me to accept that, but the others demonstrated it to me. Admiral Molina Pico doesn't talk about it, Admiral Ferrer doesn't talk about it. I write them and they don't answer. If these were acts of war and military orders, why don't they answer? I don't understand. My doubts aren't just for the sake of doubting."

"At that time, no one had a moment's doubt about the legitimacy of the orders to throw prisoners into the sea from an airplane in flight? That didn't conflict with your Christian background, your military education?"

"The few men who left the navy obviously were opposed to it. Almost all of us thought that we were traitors—I mean, that *they* were traitors."

"How many do you know of who left?"

"(Commander Jorge) Búsico and another one whose name I don't remember."

"Only two. That indicates a serious lapse in all of your educations."

"No, no, no. I don't believe so. Because if the armed forces are what they must be, you have to have total confidence in your superior officer. Perhaps it's difficult for you to understand it, but the logical thing is not to doubt your superior. If you're going to stop and analyze every single order. . ."

"But this is not a technical problem."

"No, it's not technical. But all of us were convinced that we were involved in a different kind of war, for which we were not prepared, and that we were using the means we had at hand, that the enemy continually had good information and we had to deny them that information. From the religious point of view, talked over with chaplains, it was accepted."

"The chaplains approved of the method?"

"Yes. After my first flight, despite everything I'm telling you, it was very hard for me to accept it on a personal level. After returning, although I might coldly have thought everything was fine, that was not the reality inside me. I believe all human beings have this problem; if I had had to shoot someone, I would have felt the same way. I don't think any human being takes pleasure in killing another. The next day I didn't feel very good and I was talking with the chaplain of the school, who found a Christian explanation for it. I don't know if it comforted me, but at least it made me feel better."

"What was the Christian explanation?"

"I don't remember very well, but he was telling me that it was a Christian death, because they didn't suffer, because it wasn't traumatic, that they had to be eliminated, that war was war and even the Bible provided for eliminating the weeds from the wheat field. He gave me some support."

"Other colleagues of yours were also disturbed?"

"At heart, all of us were disturbed."

"But you talked among yourselves?"

"It was taboo."

"You went, threw twenty living people into the ocean, came back, and didn't talk about it among yourselves?"

"No."

"You picked up where you had left off, as if it hadn't existed."

"Yes. Everyone wants to erase it from their minds. I can't."

"What do you think, did each one talk about it at home, with his family?"

"I don't know."

"Did you talk about it with your family?"

"Little by little. The only person I really talked it over with — little by little, because it was hard for me — was my wife. After some time had gone by, I talked about it with two civilian friends. Fundamentally, I wanted one of my superiors to tell the public what happened during that period. That is the key issue. If what I say is true, if we acted within acceptable military parameters, carrying out orders, and there is no doubt that everything was correct, why is it being hidden? But you tell me we acted as a gang.

"You acted as a gang and did things that go against the laws of war, international conventions, Christian morality, Jewish morality, Islamic morality."

"Shooting someone is immoral too. Or is it better? Who suffers more, the one who knows he is going to be shot or the one who dies by our method?"

"The right to know that he is going to die cannot be denied any human being. It is a fundamental measure of respect for human dignity, even in an extreme situation."

"I agree with you about that. If I were on the other side, I would want to know. You're right. At that time I didn't think so. I thought it was true, all that about. . ."

"Don't you think that doing it in that way betrays, apart from everything else, an enormous cowardice, avoiding the gaze of the person who is going to be killed, carrying them off happy, full of illusions, in order to be able to come back afterward and pretend nothing happened, in order not to have to remember a scream or a gaze?"

"When you put it that way, it could be. It wasn't a normal act — today I have no doubt of that. I condemn it, and not because I want to justify myself. I think it is unjustifiable. But I also think it is unjustifiable to go on hiding it. I have criticized the Mothers of the Plaza de Mayo a lot, and I've thought of them as my enemies. But if what happened to the Mothers of the Plaza de Mayo had happened to me, (their leader) Hebe Bonafini wouldn't have amounted to a hill of beans next to me."

"I don't think so. The mothers of the Plaza de Mayo are much braver than you are."

"Why do you say that?"

"Because of the life you've each lived."

"I'm saying if I were in their place."

"You would have stayed home."

"That's what *you* think."

"Yes."

"I don't agree. I don't think there could be a greater aberration for a parent than to have a disappeared child. A child is alive or dead, but there's no such thing as 'disappeared.' And that is the fault of the armed forces."

"And this did not pass through anyone's head at the time you were doing it?"

"No."

"Then apart from being a gang of criminals, you were sick. Now you're saying it in all clarity: an aberration that was the fault of the armed forces."

"That aberration is the responsibility of the armed forces and now also of the government, which must demand that they make public the list of the dead. Don't misunderstand what I am saying about the Mothers of the Plaza de Mayo. I don't know if I would have had the courage they had."

"There isn't a single member of the Argentine military who has had the courage the mothers had."

"That is your political assessment, which is irrelevant. Why do you say that?"

"Because of what the mothers did and what the military did. While you were throwing defenseless people out of airplanes, they went out under the most adverse conditions to call for justice. That is much more courageous."

"Don't misinterpret me."

"At the Navy School of Mechanics, were records kept?"

"It was perfectly structured. It was a military organization, not a gang as you say."

"It was a gang with account books."

"That's what you say."

"Did you have record books?"

"They had records of everything. It wasn't a record of dead people. It was within the military organization. Your interpretation is that ESMA was an armed group. Do you mean to separate the navy from ESMA or ESMA from the navy?"

"No."

"You're saying that the gang was the whole navy?"

"Yes."

"I agree with you on that. At that time it wasn't like that. If you say that the whole navy was involved in it, then can some be promoted and others not? Can the Senate promote some and not others? Does it have all the facts in hand with which to make that judgment? Were there one, two, or three men who tortured or killed while the rest didn't?"

"You're telling me that all of you tortured and killed?"

"No. All of us were part of the navy when that was being done, and we were rotated through different tasks. In a war, one guy cleans, another guy cooks, other guys kill. But that doesn't mean that they weren't all in the war, or in a gang, as you say and as the navy authorities make me feel by not telling the truth."

"But cooking isn't the same thing as torturing."

"When you're in a war, you don't think about that. It's the enemy. Otherwise, explain to me why the navy acted that way. At the War Academy, do they educate murderers to fight against defenseless civilians?"

"You say it in your letter: 'They made me a criminal.'"

"Because time demonstrated, with the attitudes of the superior officers when they hid all of it, that they were acting in a strange way. If you carry out orders and enough time goes by that they are no longer secret for operative reasons, and they are still being hidden or even directly lied about—as Videla did when he said that he understood that certain subversives had left the country, others might have died unidentified, and that there might have been some excesses—this is lying in a treacherous way. And in the context of that lie, I say we were transformed into criminals. Because all those of us who were subordinates within the naval organizations believed that these were serious and coherent orders. But then the truth is hidden. Why is it hidden? It's hidden when something is being done that is not appropriate. Why do you think they didn't answer my letters?"

"Because they don't have an answer to give you. You were saying that the Senate doesn't have all the facts of the case in hand. It has a lot of them and could have more, but Pernías and Rolón are the first protagonists who are beginning to talk about the facts. Until now, this was known only from the victims, the human rights organizations, and the courts. No officer had ever said in the first person what Pernías said, that torture was the tool that was used during interrogations."

"But it isn't appropriate for a commander to talk about that subject."

"All the admirals who gave the orders came before the courts and none of them admitted it."

"Why?"

"Out of cowardice. Or do you have another explanation?"

"No. So my letter is right, and we were acting like criminals."

"Of course. How did you decide to write the first letter?"

"For me, the declaration Videla made when he was released from prison with the pardon was unacceptable. I took the letter to his house personally and gave it to the guard, who signed a receipt for me. Videla never answered me. So I informed Admiral Ferrer by letter. When I got tired of getting no response from my superiors, I sent another letter, with photocopies of all the preceding ones, to the president of the nation in his role as commander-in-chief of the

armed forces. It was received by Brigadier General Andrés Antonietti, who was director of the Military House of the Presidency."

"*What happened?*"

"They never answered me. From what I know, President
Menem read the letter and said to Antonietti, 'Stop this mad-
man.' Clearly it's a difficult issue. I didn't find anyone to support
me. I spoke with other officers, but it's a very complicated issue."

"*What did you say to them?*"

"That once and for all this had to be brought to light, that the
issue had to be closed by telling the truth. Not in order to defend
ourselves or to justify ourselves, but this is the harsh reality. The
term 'disappeared' is unacceptable to me, and on top of that it
falls on my shoulders. Because I didn't make anyone disappear,
nor did anyone else in the navy. In a war, the enemy was eliminated; it could also have been done by shooting them. Who has
made them into 'the disappeared'? Those who have the responsibility for the leadership of the navy and the government. The
issue comes up again with the nonpromotion of Captains
Pernías and Rolón, which I consider to be the greatest injustice.
And I will clarify that I have not spoken personally with them for
a very long time. I don't even know what they think of my letters. When Astiz learned about my efforts to make a declaration
at the French embassy and prove that an injustice was being
committed, he sent someone to ask me not to raise a fuss,
because he had been promised that his situation would be
worked out discreetly. I never thought the silence could go so far
as to allow the Senate Confirmation Committee, for lack of
information, to commit an injustice, since it was an issue for the
entire navy; and from Admiral Massera down to the lowest lieutenant junior grade who participated, no one should be promoted if Pernías and Rolón are not promoted.

"*You're saying that all navy officers participated in kidnapping, torture, and clandestine executions?*"

"No navy officer participated in kidnapping, torture, and

clandestine eliminations. The entire navy participated in detentions, interrogations, and the elimination of the subversives,
which could have been done by various methods. You know that
it would have been ridiculous to conduct searches with a judicial
warrant; with a very basic interrogation technique we would
never have extracted any kind of information; and it would have
been the same to eliminate them by shooting them, if that were
the decision passed down through the chain of command. Not
that I want to justify myself or justify those who were there."

"You participated in torture sessions?"

"No. But I am a participant in the issue, I had no doubt that
they were going on. I saw an interrogation."

"So you participated."

"No, no, no. I observed."

*"What does that mean, to observe an interrogation? You
were part of it."*

"No, no, no, because I didn't interrogate or anything. I went
there—I watched it for a reason I'll tell you about in time."

"You had to talk to someone who was there?"

"No. It was a circumstantial matter that made me enter the
place where a person was being interrogated."

*"You wanted to listen to the interrogation, the person inter-
ested you?"*

"No, I had a personal doubt that maybe I'll tell you about later."

"You say you did not participate in torture sessions."

"But do you think that I didn't know that torture was used in
the interrogations, or do you by any chance believe there was
anyone in the navy who didn't know?"

"Knowing is one thing, participating is another."

"What's the difference? They aren't different things. If you
know it isn't right, even if you don't participate, you have to
resign, or bring it up."

*"But it isn't the same thing to know something is happening
and to do it yourself."*

"It was the normal method and all of us had taken it upon ourselves, so that the responsibility is unavoidable for all of us. It's different if you're outside and the whole thing is totally foreign to you, you don't have anything to do with it, you could denounce it. But if you're inside and you accept it, you're an accomplice. All of us, in one way or another, participated. The responsibility of those who did not participate directly can't be diminished."

"What percentage did not participate directly?"

"I don't know. Very few men participated directly in interrogations. Did you know that the guys who tortured were from the coast guard and the police?"*

"Under the attentive gaze and the orders of the gentlemen of the sea, who didn't dirty their hands with it."

"A lot of men participated in operations, as you say, in kidnappings, which were detentions, because they were rotated. Even on weekends, in addition to those who were rotated, officers came from various posts to carry out certain tasks. As for the flights, I don't know what percentage flew or did not fly."

"Torture was the specialty of a few men?"

"Of those who interrogated the prisoners. I don't think it's so easy to torture."

"For technical reasons?"

"Yes. I know of two men who interrogated. There were men who needed information, and they asked those who did the interrogations for it. But you're focusing on torture, as if only those who applied torture were responsible. Not at all. All of us bore the same responsibility. What do you want to do, justify the men who were in the navy at that time?"

---

* Scilingo's statement here does not coincide with the testimony of the former prisoners; those who wielded the weapon of choice in the dirty war were navy officers. Scilingo was unaware of this because his duties were primarily logistical and did not involve much intelligence work.

"No. I want to get a full description of what happened, to know everything you know. Everyone participated in the flights, or was that the specialty of a few people, too?"

"It was a rotating duty. I don't know if 100 percent of the navy participated, but each time there was a flight, different people went along. There are top ranking officers who participated in flights and were promoted. Why not Rolón? All of the facts must be assembled and made known, because the country must know what happened. This is the true history. Here are the living and here are the sufferers, and I have to return to the issue of the disappeared, which is aberrant. The country has done very little.

"Apart from the flights, what were your duties?"

"I was in the street. I was chief of automotive services for ESMA, in charge of 202 vehicles. Around fifty of them belonged to the navy. The others turned up. . ."

"Stolen in the street. . ."

"That's what you say. They were recuperated."

"It was also an institutional decision for those cars to turn up?"

"Of course. It's like this: if a tank was needed, a tank was found, and if a Ford Falcon was needed, a Ford Falcon was found. The objective was to destroy the enemy, by whatever means and with the materials that were required. There was a system by which all the vehicles that were needed were acquired."

"How did they get them? The officers hot-wired them in the street and drove them off?"

"Noooo. The officers didn't do that kind of work."

"The noncommissioned officers?"

"I don't know."

"What? The chief of automotive services doesn't know?"

"They brought the vehicles to me. Clearly they were not legitimately acquired vehicles. This vehicle must be transformed, repainted green. Those orders were given to me by Lieutenant Vaca—alias Lieutenant Vaca. And it was done."

"And the license plate had to be changed."

"No. The license plate was something automotive services didn't deal with. It was changed at the parking lot. That was one of Vaca's jobs. So many vehicles and spare parts were moving through that there was a lot of money at stake. The money was handled by the accounting department, but there was a lack of control. I had to find a new shop chief, who ended up becoming a noncommissioned officer in the army. Don Juan he was called, a brilliant man. He tried to put things on such a serious footing that they got out of hand. One problem was that we couldn't keep track of the vehicles by their license plates because they changed the plates permanently. It was a year like no other, what do you want me to say. Automotive services was no longer organized like a military shop, but like a civilian one. We even had Ford manuals there because of the number of Fords. Civilian personnel who were strangers to the navy were hired. This caused some problems because sometimes the vehicles arrived all bloody and the civilians weren't used to that. It was a normal shop."

"What was the F-100 Swat van, which was used for mobile torture?"

"It wasn't used for mobile torture. It wasn't like that at all."

"With bunkbeds..."

"It was for intelligence-gathering purposes. A male or female subversive almost always went along to point out people, and they had to spend hours and hours huddled up in some hiding place waiting for the person. It was a little motor home. I can tell you this because it was in the shop many times. It had air conditioning and other systems for carrying out a lengthy intelligence-gathering mission in a nonidentifiable way. But it didn't have anything for torture. Intelligence-gathering isn't torture, it's obtaining information from the enemy."

"What was your cover name?"

"I don't remember."

"I don't believe that."

"I think it was Puma, or something like that. But I'm not sure. Most of the time I was in uniform with automotive services, I had to be visible. I participated in operations, but not very many. I wasn't dressed in civilian clothes all day. Perhaps the fact that I spent so much time in uniform makes me hypercritical of some things."

"Did you also participate in operations in which people were kidnapped?"

"I participated in one. I was involved in logistical matters only, but I participated in one. You say 'kidnapped,' but then it was 'detention of persons.'"

"What was it like?"

"The van that you mentioned was there, with people who were going to finger someone. There was going to be a meeting and they identified the person who was to be arrested and he was taken prisoner."

"How was he taken prisoner?"

"When he realized what was going on, the bullets started to fly. He resisted, they had to shoot at him and he was wounded. He got a bullet in the hip. I was the one who had to drive him in an ambulance to the naval hospital, where they operated on him to remove the bullet."

"Afterward what happened to that person?"

"I don't know what happened. He was probably interrogated and the rest."

"You don't know who he is?"

"I think he's the leader of the cell that tried to blow up the presidential airplane. I had a chance to talk to him in the ambulance. It was a conversation between two confirmed enemies. I don't know which of us was more convinced of what he was doing. He was very firm, very serious. Someone to be respected. He always stayed in my mind. I think he was a diver, and from what he said then he had been trained at Puerto Madryn (in the extreme south of Argentina)."

"How old was he?"

"In his early thirties."

"From your description, he could be Alfredo Nicoletti, who was arrested last year with the supergang after having robbed an armored car."

He looks at the tape recorder. He sees that it's running, and only makes a gesture with his thumb toward the ceiling, while shaking his head. He hesitates before deciding to leave his words on the tape.

"I don't think it could be him, because afterward he disappeared. So much guilt is placed on Astiz, but the group delivers the prisoner there and doesn't know what happens afterward. . ."

He tried to change the subject.

"You did know what happened. You did know that they were interrogated with torture and then thrown out of airplanes."

"Yes, but what I mean is that Astiz. . . What is he being accused of? Of having kidnapped, tortured, and killed. You realize that it was the Argentine navy that detained, interrogated, and eliminated. The prisoner is handed over in Dorado, and from then on the intelligence people take over, to interrogate him and the rest."

"If the navy were to inform the confirmation committee of everything, what do you think would happen? Would they say, 'Ah, no, if that's how it is then we have to promote Pernías and Astiz'?"

"They may say no, but then they would have to evaluate him along with the others. They can't have a double standard."

"What standard do you think they should employ?"

"I don't know. Let the confirmation committee decide. Either all of them go or all of them are promoted. It's that simple."

"And what do you think, should they all go or should they all be promoted?"

"It doesn't make sense for all of them to go."

"So all of them would have to be promoted?"

"All those who passed through the normal screening procedures should be promoted. They should not be held up because
of political problems."

*"But this is not a political problem. They would have to pro-
mote all of those who participated?"*

"What's the difference between Lieutenant X and Lieutenant
Rolón?"

"You're the one who knows."

"There is none. At some moment Rolón's name was leaked,
but there are others who may have done worse things, from the
human point of view, let's say. Rolón was in the intelligence
office. I doubt whether he ever made a flight. Who is going to
measure this? The confirmation committee could, if it had all
the evidence in hand. You saw that the two of them went to
make their declaration alone. That struck me. Someone must
have decided to do it that way. I can't imagine a similar case in
the army, a lieutenant colonel going alone and out of uniform to
make a declaration before the confirmation committee without a
superior officer at his side to advise him. It lends credence to
what you are saying, that they were all gangsters. These are
things that cause me so much doubt that I don't know who is
right, you or me."

*"To get rid of the gang, what rank would be the dividing
line?"*

"Commander."

"From commander on up, they all participated."

"Yes."

*"What operative consequences would it have to retire them
all?"*

"I don't think that beheading an armed force in such a traumatic way would be very logical."

*"You believe that it must be established that all of them
participated and consequently no one can be sanctioned."*

"I can't even state an opinion about a decision like that. It completely exceeds what I can say. It should be analyzed at the highest political level."

"But what is your motivation? In one of your letters, you offer to make a declaration on Astiz's behalf at the French embassy."

"Astiz was a lieutenant junior grade. He was carrying out orders. As much of a gang as you say there was, it's unthinkable that a lieutenant junior grade could have made decisions like those attributed to Astiz. He was carrying out orders—we can't call him a gangster. No one went to tell the French courts the truth."

"Astiz didn't tell the truth either."

"He would have been held prisoner there."

"He could have said it here."

"Astiz cannot make a public declaration. He's on active duty, he has to ask for authorization."

"But he was put on trial in Argentina and he made a declaration."

"They must have given him orders about what he had to say. Because the gang, as you say, which for me is not a gang at all, was managed that way, by authorizations, carrying out orders. You see that I am asking for authorization."

"And no one answers you."

"Do you know why they didn't pardon Astiz? Because he infiltrated the Mothers of the Plaza de Mayo. But you have to have balls to do that."

"To hand over a dozen old women and nuns you don't need any courage at all, it's an act of cowardice."

"But do you know what they would have done to him if he had been discovered?"

"They would have thrown him out of the group. What courage did he need to hand them over?"

"But, were they alone? If you are given the order to infiltrate a certain place in order to determine certain things. . . For you, nothing was happening in the country?"

"But what possible risk was Mr. Astiz running by infiltrating a group of family members of disappeared persons who were collecting money in order to publish a notice in the newspaper at Christmas, trying to reconstruct, with all the difficulties faced by those who do not have the power that you people had, the list of the disappeared that you yourself say the gang should have published?"

"No, not the gang, the navy. I say that now, but at that moment perhaps it wasn't appropriate to publish it. So many unconventional methods were used because the war was not conventional. It was a matter of withholding information from the enemy, creating uncertainty as to what had happened to their prisoners, or what you call abductees. The logical thing would have been to inform the public of what happened and who the dead were before President Alfonsín took power. Information doesn't bring anything to an end. It won't bring back to life those who died on either side. There may be wounds, and who knows how much time it will take for them to close. However many amnesty laws are passed, by decree or by communiqué, this issue is not resolved. But how different it would have been if the truth had been known, if the disappeared had been eliminated by being transformed into the dead. Do you remember who said that the disappeared did not exist? (The former president of the Radical Civic Union, Ricardo) Balbín. Balbín said, 'What disappeared? They're all dead.' Nevertheless, they remain the disappeared."

"If Astiz had been discovered as he was infiltrating the Church of the Holy Cross, what do you think would have happened?"

"They could have killed him."

"Who?"

"What do you mean, who?"

"The nuns?"

"No, no, but do you think they were alone, alone, alone?"

"And what do you think?"

"I think that the subversive groups were supporting them."

"Supporting them? How? Do you believe they were a military organization equal to yours? It appears to me that you have a very distorted vision of the facts. Many years have gone by and there hasn't been a single instance of personal vengeance against anyone."

"But some members of the military were kidnapped at that time."

"How many?"

"I don't know."

"Two, three cases. General Pita, Lieutenant Colonel Del Valle Larrabure, Admiral Alemán, who else?"

"The next time we see each other I'll see if I can get some information about this. I have it at home."

"What were the personal and corporate-financial mistakes you say you made out of excessive pride when you left the navy?"

"I got involved with some people who. . . But because I was starving to death."

"Were you convicted of anything?"

"Yes. Fraud."

"What happened?"

"When I retired, I launched the first big video rental store in Bahía Blanca (the city in the province of Buenos Aires where the largest naval base is located). After that I set up the first cable television system, with some members of my family. My economic situation improved enormously, very rapidly, and as quickly as I rose, I fell. I was ruined and from there I kind of stumbled around until I recuperated."

"What was the conviction of fraud for?"

"I was in Buenos Aires, and I introduced a civilian friend to a company that produced videos. He paid for seven video cassettes with a check postdated thirty days later. And they discovered that the account, which was in his name, was closed. They charged me as his accomplice. I paid for the seven video cassettes, but the trial went on. The defense lawyer asked in Bahía Blanca for docu-

ments certifying that I was the owner of a video rental store, but
the registries for the whole province are in the city of La Plata,
and the judge sentenced me stating that I was never able to prove
that I was the owner of a video company. But now I have received
all the documentation from La Plata, and I'm going to present it
and request that the matter be reconsidered."

*"When this is published, the brave men of the navy are going
to respond to it by discrediting you on the basis of that conviction. You know that?"*

"Yes. That's one of the reasons I hesitated to talk. But
between one thing and another, I feel better talking."

He covered the microphone with his hand. It was harder for
him to talk about the fraud than about the flights. He preferred
to go on talking about ESMA.

"Was there another method of eliminating the prisoners?"

"They say that the athletic field is filled with the bodies of guerrillas, and that's wrong. It may be that the corpse of some wounded
person who couldn't take it and died was cremated there."

"In what way?"

"They burned it. That's another topic that made the rounds. I
had problems about that with the civilian personnel under me.
They realized something strange was going on, because the
Dorado people would ask for old tires in order to cremate the
body. That was another way. But there were very few of them."

"How many?"

"Very few."

*"In other words, they were taken up in airplanes when they
were capable of walking."*

"They were always capable of walking. Those who were
wounded were treated."

"But in the cases you mention, the wounded could not. . ."

"Not wounded, no, dead. They arrived wounded. They were
arrested and resisted arrest and sometimes they didn't survive,
like anyone wounded in a war."

"Was there some special place for this?"

"No, no. Behind. But these were very rare cases."

"Did they have some special installation?"

"No, there was never anything out of the ordinary. What's more, the athletic field was always in use. It was never shut down."

"They burned a body and then played soccer on the athletic field?"

"Nooooo. That athletic field is very big. It's on land reclaimed from the river. The farthest part is practically inaccessible, it's not in use. It's behind everything, next to the river."

The tape has run out. But he doesn't get up. He asks me to put in another cassette. There is still something he wants to say.

Chapter Four
Shadowlands

HE HAD by now made several brief forays toward them, yet without fully revealing his worst memories. But he had come close enough and did not want to pull back, as if confession would be a kind of grim relief. He brought up the question spontaneously, as we were speaking of something else.

"You asked me what happened in the airplanes. Once the plane had taken off, the doctor on board gave them a second dose of an extremely powerful tranquilizer. It put them into a deep sleep."

"When the prisoners went to sleep, what did you do?"

"This is very sick."

"What's sick is what you people did."

"I would not want anyone to think it gives me pleasure to talk about this."

"You've already made it clear that you want to talk about Rolón and Astiz. I'm asking you about the details of the flight, so it won't remain an abstraction."

"There are four things that give me a very bad time. The two flights I did, the person I saw tortured, and the memory of the chains and shackles that were put on the prisoners. I barely saw them a couple of times, but I cannot forget that sound. I don't want to talk about it. Let me go."

"This is not ESMA. You're here of your own free will and you can go whenever you want to."

"Yes, I know. I didn't mean to say that. There are details that are important, but it's hard for me to tell you about them. I think about them and they make me crazy. In their unconscious state, the prisoners were stripped, and when the commander of the airplane gave the order, which happened according to where the plane was, the hatch was opened and they were thrown out, naked, one by one. That's the story. A gruesome story, but true, and no one can deny it. I can't get rid of the image of the naked bodies lined up in the plane's aisle, like something in a movie about Nazis. It was done from Skyvan planes belonging to the coast guard and Electras belonging to the navy. In the Skyvan, it was through the rear hatch, which slides down to open. It's a big door, but it has no intermediate positions. It's closed or it's open, so it was kept in the open position. The noncommissioned officer kept his foot on the door, so that there would be about 40 centimeters opening onto empty space. Then we started to lower the subversives through there. I was pretty nervous about the situation I was experiencing and I almost fell out into empty space.

"How?"

"I slipped and they caught me."

"You mentioned two flights in the same month."

"Yes, in June or July of 1977. The second flight was on a Saturday. My family was living in Bahía Blanca and I went there every two weeks, so I worked on Saturday and Sunday. I was at the school. They gave me the order. They put me in command of the convoy and we went through the same steps. This time it was

an Electra. The procedure was the same, but through the emer-
gency door in the stern, on the starboard side—I mean on the
right. This door was removed, and the operative who was to
carry out the task was secured with a rope. On this second flight,
in keeping with the way the navy saw things then, there were
also special guests."

"*What does that mean, 'special guests?'*"

"Upper echelon navy officers who didn't participate because
they were only on the flight to back us up. For example, captains, high-ranking officers who were posted elsewhere."

"*And what did they do?*"

"Nothing. It was a way of lending their moral support to the
task we were doing."

"*Were they seated next to the prisoners?*"

"No, no. There were hardly any seats. There was a small
group of seats toward the front and the rest was empty."

"*And where were the high-ranking officers?*"

"They were seated and then, during the operation, they stood
up and watched."

"*They were watching.*"

"Yes, yes. They were watching."

"*But they did not participate.*"

"Well, to say they weren't participating... "

"*Obviously they were participating and that was the meaning
of their presence.*"

"Of course."

"*Why didn't they get involved actively, with their own
hands?*"

"Because it wasn't necessary."

"*How were the unconscious people taken to the door?*"

"Between two men."

"*They were dragged?*"

"They were carried to the door."

"*They remained unconscious.*"

"Totally unconscious. No one suffered in the least."

"There was never any exception to that?"

This question seems to disturb him more than the others. He thinks and thinks again before answering.

"No, none I can attest to."

"You never saw anyone wake up?"

"Anyone. . . ?"

"Wake up."

"No, I never saw that."

"Anyone resisting?"

"No, no, no."

"And why did you slip?"

"I slipped because the floor of the plane is made of metal and I almost went down, I was working hard pushing the bodies of subversives."

"Was any study made to determine in what place—"

"I'm sure there must have been some studies. I imagine there were. Out on the open ocean."

"How many people do you calculate were killed in this way?"

"Between fifteen and twenty per Wednesday."

"For how long?"

"Two years."

"Two years, a hundred Wednesdays, from fifteen hundred to two thousand people."

"Yes. As we left the airport, a flight plan was filed for the Punta Indio base. When we reached Punta Indio, the plane veered out to sea. Someone said that the flight plans from that period had disappeared, something else that seems barbaric to me. At that time it may have been, but now, I don't know."

"What navy personnel went along on every flight?"

"The plane's normal crew was in the cockpit."

"And with the prisoners?"

"Two officers, one noncommissioned officer, a petty officer, and the doctor. On my first flight, the petty officer, who was from the coast guard, was completely unaware of what the mission was. When he realized on board what he had to do, he had a nervous breakdown. He started weeping. He didn't understand anything, his words were all jumbled up. It started making me nervous, too. I started to explain to him, and I told the noncommissioned officer to speak to the pilots, because it was becoming quite a situation by then. . . I didn't know how to handle a coast guard man in such a critical situation. In the end, they sent him to the cockpit. The Skyvan is a big box, with a separate cockpit. We finished undressing the subversives—"

"You, Lieutenant Vaca, the doctor—"

"No, no. The doctor gave them the second injection, nothing more. Then he went to the cockpit. That happened on the second flight too."

"Why?"

"They said it was because of the Hippocratic oath. I think it was that way on all the flights. They said that was the reason, and in some way it was reasonably well accepted. Let's be concrete. The commander of one of those planes flew the plane. The pilot and copilot were flying the plane. Let's use your terms. They didn't kidnap, they didn't torture, they didn't kill?"

"How can you say they didn't?"

"According to you, the guilty one is only the one who's there, inside the problem, the one who is torturing. What's the difference between the plane's pilot and Rolón and Pernías?"

"There's no difference."

"Ahhhh. So, none of them or all of them, within the navy's standard screening procedures, but once they've passed through those screening procedures, none of them or all of them. Do you agree with me or not? Maybe you'll tell me 'None of them.' But it's got to be none or all."

"All those who participated. The one who was piloting the plane in which those people were killed was participating. The cook was not participating."

"The cook is a bad example."

"You're the one who used it."

"No, not the cook, because we're talking about the leaders and the officers on active duty at that time."

"What you're telling me is that they either participated in kidnapping, or they participated in torture, or they participated in clandestine executions. There wasn't anyone who didn't participate in any of those three things?"

"Perhaps, by chance, someone did not participate. Everyone was rotated. Someone might appear who could say, 'I wasn't there.' But he knew about it, and if he didn't participate it wasn't because he didn't want to, but because he wasn't assigned to. Make no mistake about that."

"What you're suggesting is that the burden of proof would have to be inverted; starting from the basis that everyone participated, and then analyzing in each specific case who can demonstrate that he did not?"

"If someone wants to justify himself, let him justify himself. It could be. It's an analysis you made, but we'd have to see if anyone wants to justify himself. It may be that someone might appear who would want to."

"If that were the political decision, a whole lot of men would appear and try to justify themselves."

"That could be the solution. It could be. But as things stand, it's unfair."

"To whom?"

"It's unfair that those who were truly active participants have already been approved by the Senate Confirmation Committee. What is the difference between Admiral Arduino who gave me the order and Captain Rolón? And Arduino ended up as chief of naval operations, under a constitutional government, after passing before the Senate Confirmation Committee. We must not be hypocritical. We must tell the truth. This is history. And on the basis of the truth, let decisions be made. You ask me what I would do. I wouldn't do anything. First of all, I'm not on active duty, and second, I'm not a politician. What I say is, gentlemen, enough. Let's tell the truth, and on the basis of the truth, let them decide what they have to decide. But it's a lie to go on playing hide and seek and suddenly someone appears who isn't promoted because they say he was a torturer. He isn't promoted because the truth is not being told. Who are they protecting by not telling the truth?"

"You say you don't want to participate in a cover-up. A cover-up of what?"

"Of hiding something, of withholding information—and not only from the confirmation committee. They are withholding information about the disappeared from society."

"If everyone participated, they aren't all part of a cover-up. They are all participants in a crime. They are guilty of homicides, not cover-ups."

"Who is it who's covering something up?"

"You say that they are engaged in a cover-up."

"Who is it who should have given out the information? Or do you think it is normal for a commander to go and try to defend himself before the Senate Confirmation Committee by saying what the method was? It had a tremendous impact. You saw the headlines in all the newspapers. They went to defend themselves in a matter they know at heart is an injustice. And what did they say? Did the two officers who went to talk with the confirmation committee lie or did they tell the truth?"

"They told part of the truth."

"They weren't asked for all of it. Are they the ones who have to tell it?"

"If they had been asked about the clandestine executions they would have talked about them?"

"I don't know. They weren't asked. But do things have to come to that point or does the truth have to be told once and for all? Don't you think it's time for this to be brought to light, finally and clearly? My information is minimal. Or do you think that if I had the names of the disappeared I would have kept them to myself. But I don't have them."

"When you made those transports, did you know who those people were?"

"I had no idea."

"You didn't meet them beforehand? You hadn't seen them at ESMA?"

"No, no. Nor did it interest me. I was placing total faith in the decisions my superiors had made."

"But, in the line of duty, you didn't come into contact . . . ?"

"No, no, I only had occasional contact with the prisoners."

"What kind of contact?"

"Not talking to them. Just seeing them, and the rest. There was no direct interaction. A rumor had it that the ex-navy man Jorge Devoto was thrown out while conscious, but I never knew if it was true."

"You didn't know who the prisoners were?"

"No, but neither did I try to find out. I never had a single doubt about what was being done there. If you want me to tell you—look, I don't . . . I would be lying to you completely."

"I don't want you to tell me that."

"I didn't have the least doubt about what was taking place in a totally legal way, as was fitting. I was twenty-eight years old and had spent ten years in the navy. It's neither a lot nor a little. I was a lieutenant and was sufficiently trained and had enough seniority not to have doubts about my superiors. I was totally absorbed in my career."

"The issue is not doubting your superiors. But, in the education that you men were given . . ."

"That didn't exist. What did exist was killing the enemy."

"How is the enemy to be killed?"

"In war. That was a dirty war, for which we were unprepared."

"Is it true that you were unprepared or is that an excuse?"

"We were not prepared for that."

"From 1958 on, the naval intelligence service was working on the hypothesis, giving courses, publishing articles, pamphlets, books, giving people special training . . ."

"Whatever you like, but that has nothing to do with the real preparation of the men of the navy for the fight against subversion. Or do you think that they were giving courses on how to fight in the street? After it began, when the combat began, but before that no. If Rolón were a marine infantryman — but he's a naval officer."

"Pernías?"

"Pernías is an infantryman. There were airmen, too. Is any airman prepared to fight against subversion in the street?"

"Perhaps certain branches were not, but the navy as an institution was preparing for it for twenty years."

"Ideological preparation is one thing, but what does it have to do with anything? What there was were attempts to counteract the ideological penetration of the Left. If you ask me what was being done about that at the highest levels of the navy, I don't know. Ah, you are saying that as a result of that, we were convinced."

"Prepared. I have the testimony of an officer who was instructed on how to torture."

"In the navy?"

"Yes. An officer at ESMA. During an antisubversive exercise, they tortured each other. The army's officers did the same thing."

"I never heard that. Maybe the marine infantry."

"It seems to me that it's the reverse of what you think. They had been prepared for what they did. That's why no one had any doubts."

Every time an idea surprises him, he remains silent. He resists accepting a different perspective, but he isn't categorical either. "That's your analysis, that's what you say, it may be, perhaps you are right," he says as he resumes the dialogue each time, with a flexibility that seems strange in such an institutionalized personality.

"That's an analysis you can make. I don't know. If the order
had been to go out and kill Chileans or subversives, it would
have been accepted in the same way. Superior orders are not
open to discussion. If you start having doubts . . . I can have
doubts about my superiors once they don't answer letters that
are clearly written. Why don't they answer me? You're convinced that the navy acted as a gang, and I don't want to be convinced. But facts like those make me wonder. Admiral Ferrer
doesn't answer me, Admiral Molina Pico doesn't answer me.
The silence continues. I don't know. I even tried to get a feel for
what is going on inside the navy, and no one knows what happened. I don't want to be a hypocrite and say, 'I'm the good guy
now because I'm talking about this.' No. Because tomorrow
they're going to say, 'Scilingo, the repentant one.' And that's not
how it is. Scilingo, under the same circumstances, would have
done exactly the same thing. But everything has been changing,
and instead of being recounted as a triumph, I'm telling you
about it in a situation I can't even describe, thanks to my superiors . . . And fundamentally thanks to me, also. Because I believed
absolutely in everything I was doing and carried out all the
orders with complete conviction. That's the dirty war we won."

Dusk has invaded the room. Time has stopped. When the
light is switched on, Scilingo looks at his watch. He's grown tac-
iturn. It's hard for him to go back to the shadowland of his memory. He says good-bye without arranging for another meeting.

Chapter Five
Just Like Reality

SCILINGO'S VOICE is still there on the tape, the documents still bear his signature. At his house, they answer the telephone and pass it over to him, and the same voice that is on the tape comes across the wire. This has happened; it's not a dream. But is it going to vanish like a dream?

When a secret kept for almost twenty years became unbearable, he told his ghastly stories to someone who only by chance was not his victim. He answered all the questions, he submitted to a role he had not imagined playing. How would he react after letting it all out, when he began to measure the step he had taken and its consequences? Would he go back to take refuge in the old institutional certainties, cut off all contact, try to prevent publication?

Not at all. Ten days later he was prepared to go on talking.

"When you decide to publish this, please give me at least twenty-four hours' notice. I know I'm putting myself in the middle of a very big mess, and I have to take certain precautions."

"Because of the navy?"

"No. Videla's group. They're the only ones who are still organized. They're a group of Catholic fanatics."

Nevertheless, he seemed calm.

"Though you might not believe it, talking has been good for me. I felt better. But you're very close-mouthed. You don't tell me what you think."

"You said that in addition to your wife you had spoken with two civilian friends about this. When?"

"Six years afterward."

"Why did you tell them about it?"

"Out of the same need that's making me talk to you about it now. At that point I wanted to know what someone who was outside of what I experienced would think of it. In some way, I think they knew about it, the way a lot of people know about it, but it's never spoken of. The subject is still taboo. I think the time has come to speak the truth. There are moments like this in each person's life. I don't know how the others are going to react or if many of them are going to be in agreement with my coming forward to describe this."

"How did your friends react?"

"In silence. They understood what I had done. It wasn't a conversation to ask for forgiveness or offer explanations. I also talked to my mother before she died.

"How did those conversations go?"

"She asked questions. I think she related it to the subject of my retirement. I never explained it to her directly, but she suspected. So she tried to find out what the problem was and to give me some support as a mother. I got aggressive with her, because I didn't want to discuss the subject. At certain stressful moments, the flights come back to my mind automatically. I've had periods when I had to take sleeping pills, periods when I drank too much. I don't think it has affected the navy, but it certainly has affected my family. It affected me profoundly. The navy cannot accept that I have this kind of problem."

"Do your children know?"

"My wife told them about it gradually. And recently I spoke with them. My fifteen-year-old daughter has a civics professor who addressed the subject. Well, in a balanced way the teacher said that the subversives were setting off bombs and that the armed forces also committed barbaric acts to stop them. In order to talk to my daughter about it, I looked for some things I have in my library. I consulted the pamphlet the armed forces published on the war against subversion and it made me ashamed. There were very few abductions of members of the military, you were right. I also showed her the magazine in which (former guerrilla chief Mario) Firmenich tells how they killed (ex-military dictator Pedro Eugenio) Aramburu (in 1970). My daughter knows everything that happened—she isn't forgetting about the bombs or anything. But when she has to tally it all up, she tells me that the armed forces did worse things. When you talk about a gang I don't agree, but with that word you leave me on a dead-end street, because a moment comes when I can't find any explanation for it. I don't know if the navy acted as a gang or as an armed force. Or if we acted in the belief that we were an armed force and in fact we were acting as a gang. And the current silence in some way justifies your position. Up until the moment of the pardons, I felt that I had carried out orders and that the sentence passed on my commanding officers was political. But all of that collapsed on me when they agreed to go quietly back to their homes and Videla started talking nonsense. It affected me tremendously. I realized that something was not right. What I had done, was it right or was it wrong?"

"Up until that moment, you had never questioned yourself?"

"It's not that I hadn't questioned myself as a human being. I hadn't questioned militarily."

"What's the difference?"

"As a human being, face to face with the enemy, when you kill you have to question it. I told you that I came back from the first flight feeling bad. Bad. I did not feel good, but I did not doubt that militarily I had carried out an order I was completely convinced about. But what happens when you discover that your commanding officers go quietly home and accept—'O.K., that's fine, they sentenced me, now they are pardoning me?' Does that mean the sentence was justified? If they had rejected the pardon, I would have thought, militarily, the political game goes on, but those men are conducting themselves fittingly. But to go home as they did, that I do not accept. Not only do I not accept it, but every time I think about it, I feel bad because it makes me question everything I did at the Navy School of Mechanics. Maybe if the former commanders in chief were still prisoners because they had not accepted the pardon, you would still see it the way you do now. I wouldn't.

"The only person who didn't accept the pardon was Graciela Daleo, a former prisoner at ESMA."

"You see. Mistaken or not, she had her convictions and still has them. And Videla, does he have any convictions about what he did, or did he just go home? They solved their personal problem and forgot about all the men who carried out their orders."

"Have you decided to talk about the tortures you witnessed?"

"One day I was in the officer's lounge at the school, near the bar, and in came the so-called Lieutenant Vaca and told me he had had a woman lawyer arrested in an investigation he had carried out personally. He told me they were interrogating her at that very moment, if I wanted to go. I went because I wanted to see what kind of investigation Lieutenant Vaca could have carried out; I had serious doubts about him. She was being interrogated with the methods that, as was said in Congress, were the methods that were used . . . In other words, she was being tortured with an electric cattle prod. I was there a very short time, first of all because . . . I don't know if I'm not . . . a little soft for that kind of thing . . . It was a woman. From what I heard from the people who were interrogating her, she had absolutely nothing to do with anything. I left. I asked about it a while later and she had disappeared.

"She had disappeared. What does that mean?"

"That she had disappeared. So then . . ."

"That they had made her disappear."

"They had . . . she had disappeared, yes. And I asked Vaca, 'but if she had nothing to do with anything . . . ?' No, no, he says, it was determined later that she had been involved in some very serious things. I always had my doubts. I don't know any more about it. But I always had my doubts. It's hard for me to tell you about it. It's real, it's like that, that's how it is. But in our discussions, when you talk about a gang and I deny it totally, these are the facts that make me wonder if there weren't gang attitudes."

"Well, to begin with, there was the commander in chief who went out boating with his mistress's husband one afternoon and came back alone."

"What do you mean, came back alone?"

"He threw him into the ocean."

"Ahhh, in the . . ."

"It was the businessman, Fernando Branca, his mistress's husband."

Scilingo doesn't answer. Like the subjects of the lack of control over the money from the auto shop or his conviction for fraud, the reference to the reason Massera was arrested during the dictatorship—by a judge appointed by the military government— seems to disturb him more than the memory of the flights.

"That kind of man was the commander in chief of the navy."

"You know, I had blind faith in Admiral . . . in then-admiral Massera. It was more than that, I had total and absolute admiration for Admiral Massera. The year after I was at the Navy School of Mechanics, I was reassigned to the frigate *Libertad*, there was a dinner before weighing anchor, and by chance I was seated next to Admiral Massera. You cannot imagine how proud I was. That's how it is. After having been an admiral, he accepted a pardon, he left in silence, and he forgot all of us who were beneath him. So, OK. What can you do?"

"*You underwent psychiatric treatment?*"

"I went several times to the psychologist at the naval hospital, who gave me a sedative. But the psychologist was a civilian and he didn't want to get involved in the issue either. Afterward he tried to steer me into therapy on the couch with a very young woman who was there. Then I said, this isn't doing any good, and I stopped going."

"*Did you read the report entitled* Nunca Más, *written by the National Commission on the Disappeared?*"

"I didn't read it impartially. I saw it as the biased publication of an enemy. Maybe I should reread it now."

"*It speaks of exactly the same thing you lived through.*"

"I always believed that the trial of the former military leaders was political. Because I was convinced of everything that was done. At that time I thought that (the head of the commission, the writer Ernesto) Sábato was a subversive, and now I realize that was ridiculous. Sábato!"

"*And what do you think of* Nunca Más *and the trial now?*"

"They both seem unimportant compared with the fact of having carried out the orders of people who have deceived me."

"*So you are still just as arrogant. The only important thing would be for your leaders to assume their responsibility. The bravery of the survivors who narrated what took place, of the members of the commission and the judges who reconstructed the truth . . .*"

"What bravery? We were under a democratic government."

"*The armed forces were still threatening, resisting the trials.*"

"The armed forces were not threatening. The proof is that the trial took place."

"*Everything civilians do seems trivial to you, it doesn't matter to you.*"

"Does it seem like a small thing to you that the military leaders do not assume responsibility for what we did?"

"*It seems like a big thing. Furthermore, it isn't only the lead-*

ers. No one on any level assumed any kind of responsibility. But I don't understand why everything apart from that seems unimportant to you."

"To retell what happened is unimportant, because it's real. The conviction of the military leaders was based on concrete facts."

"Then why did you think it was political?"

"Because at that time I was convinced."

"The subject of the flights is addressed on page 235 of (the Argentine edition of) Nunca Más *and it appeared in the testimony given during the trials. What did you feel when you learned about that?"*

"That it was a narration of the facts given by people whose ideas I did not share. It's real, just like reality. What seems aberrant to me is that my superiors don't say it. I'm still shocked by that attitude. I see the other side of it as minor."

There isn't much left to say. He's anxious and euphoric. But he has one doubt: "When you write about this, are you going to destroy me?" he asks.

"I'm going to express my opinion as little as possible."

Part II
Denial

Chapter Six
The Institutional Lie

THE SILENCE that Pernías and Rolón began to breach in the Senate had been constructed very deliberately. But Scilingo's confession finally broke through to the heart of the matter after almost two decades. It seems worthwhile to go back over the itinerary—from the initial phase of complete denial to the subsequent period of partial admissions and euphemisms—that led from the institutional lie to the truth of a lone man to whom no one wanted to listen.

Not long after the 1976 military coup, Admiral Massera, the commander in chief of the navy, had defined the lines of battle: "Those who are on the side of death and we who are on the side of life." He began by saying, "We will not have death roaming freely through Argentina," and ended with this warning: "We are not going to fight to the death; we are going to fight to victory, whether it lies before or beyond death." In between, he described the military's battle with political "subversives" as an oblique, primitive and cruel war in which "a machine of horror was unleashing its impunity on innocent and unprepared people."

In 1977, at which time more than half of the military regime's kidnappings and homicides had already taken place, President Videla spoke for the first time about the disappeared, whose existence until then had been denied and ascribed to propaganda disseminated by the country's perverse and powerful enemies. In a dialogue with foreign journalists, he described four types of *desaparecidos*: those who were living underground, traitors who had been eliminated by the guerrillas themselves, those whose bodies were left unrecognizable by fires and explosions during confrontations between the two sides, and, finally, those who had endured "excesses" committed by the military repression. He refrained from stating how many people might belong in each category and refused to discuss any specific cases.

A few days later, the chief of staff of the army, General Roberto Viola, explained in the guildhall of the country's major landowners and cattle breeders that about seven or eight thousand subversives had been arrested or killed in combat, an astonishingly imprecise figure, considering that the life or death of thousands of people was concerned. Viola was playing with numbers, Massera with words. Each one in his own way was mocking his interlocutors. One journalist said to Massera: "Information has reached us from abroad that human rights are probably not being sufficiently respected in Argentina, and it has even been said that there are people who have been unjustly deprived of their freedom or even of their lives."

"What doubt can there be that human rights are not respected in Argentina, that people are unjustly deprived of liberty and murders are committed? Otherwise, what is the meaning of the lengthy, the immense list of members of the armed forces, business people, community leaders, and people completely outside of politics, women and children, killed without pity or kept for months in so-called people's jails under conditions that would be insulting to the most despicable animal?" Massera responded. His questioner did not even think of asking him which animals he most despised.

According to Viola, losing the war was worse than dying. The only explanation the army gave the country would be to say that it had fulfilled its mission. In an insidious phrase, he referred to the losses, the deaths, the wounded, the prisoners, and what he called "those who were absent forever." So that no one would press the issue, he repeated that explanations should not be sought because none would be given.

In 1979, the Inter-American Commission on Human Rights of the Organization of American States (OAS) visited jails and interviewed politicians, members of the military, labor union leaders, businessmen, members of the media, and the families of disappeared people, gathering evidence and testimony. During the same period, General Albano Harguindeguy, then minister of the interior, boasted with an arrogance that was in its final days that Argentina confesses its sins only before God, and triumphant armies are not put on trial or asked to account for their actions after the war.

When Viola left the ranks of the army in preparation for his presidential candidacy, he said that there was one fundamental condition for the transition to democracy: the armed forces would never agree to a review of their actions, because to allow those who fought with honor and sacrifice to be placed on trial would amount to a betrayal and an insult under their code of ethics. During a visit to the United States to meet president-elect Ronald Reagan, Viola stated his conviction that military victory exempted the victor from all responsibility, and went on to say that if Germany had won World War II, the Nuremberg trials would have taken place in Virginia, thus unwittingly placing the Argentine dictatorship on an equal footing with the Nazis.

The man who replaced Viola in the army, General Leopoldo Galtieri, maintained that the military had preserved the integrity of the nation, which justified the means that had been employed. "Don't ask us for explanations, because we will not give them, just as our enemies would not have given any if they had won the war," he thundered. President Videla declared that the participation of the country's political parties in the dialogue convened by the government constituted a formal legitimization of the military's assault on power and that the participants in the dialogue had committed themselves to communicating to the public their approval of everything done during the fight against subversion.

By now, the military leaders were no longer denying the accusations or resorting to unlikely explanations of the disappearances. They were justifying them and making an acknowledgment of that justification a sine qua non for the politicians who aspired to sit down at their magnanimous table. But they were still talking about the disappearances in shameful euphemisms.

The OAS report, which came out in 1980, stated that the thousands of disappeared persons had been killed by official forces. The report also considered the appalling, systematic use of torture to be irrefutable. In the official response to that report, the military's new position crystallized. The government claimed that the risk of a national collapse had created an urgent situation in which the state had exercised its powers of self-defense and had resorted to "the appropriate means." Not to have done so would have doomed it to powerlessness and would have been a form of suicide. But the government continued to keep silent about the nature of the methods employed, a subject that remained absolutely taboo.

This problem, which the four first military juntas had underestimated at the apogee of their power, remained pressing in a way no military man would have suspected was possible after the junta lost the war with Great Britain for the Falkland (Malvinas) Islands and subsequently collapsed. The last dictator, General Benito Bignone, was responsible for organizing the withdrawal of the military from power. Before taking office, in 1982, he met with representatives of all the political parties, and only Francisco Manrique, a conservative and former naval captain, dared to suggest that it would be appropriate to publish the list of the disappeared. Bignone said that there was no such list, and no one pressed him any further.

Terrified by the possible social consequences of the regime's dissolution, the Catholic Church proposed holding a mass for reconciliation, so that the political parties could agree with the military government on the conditions of succession and negotiate an amnesty. Factions within the military vetoed an exchange of impunity for a favorable electoral timetable. But once the military had established that elections would take place within a time period that would allow the political parties to recondition their rusty machinery, the opposition politicians did not display any interest in agreeing on anything with a regime that was coming apart at the seams.

In the absence of a negotiated agreement, the military government unilaterally published a set of conditions, which principally demanded that the dirty war and the dirty business conducted by the military not be reviewed, that the judges permanently appointed by the dictatorship not be dismissed, and that the armed forces' participation in the next government be guaranteed.

In September 1983, the military Holy Trinity, made up of the chiefs of staff of the three armed forces, signed its "Final Document of the Military Junta on the War against Subversion and Terrorism." The document maintained that the cellular organization and compartmentalization of the enemy required unusual procedures such as those used during the dirty war. Since the military forces were acting on estimations that had to be made in the midst of the fight, with the degree of passion generated by combat and the defense of one's own life, "within that almost apocalyptic context, mistakes were made that, as happens in all wartime conflict, could cross the limits of respect for fundamental rights." Such errors should remain subject to the judgment of God and the compassion of mankind. They were committed while operating institutionally and within the natural chain of command in fulfillment of orders that arose from the essence of the military's task, it said.

On the subject of the disappeared, the junta accepted as a simple hypothesis that they may have died violently during battles with legal forces and that they were buried without having been identified.

Another document, solemnly entitled "Institutional Declaration," repeated that all operations were executed in accordance with plans that were approved and supervised by the high command. There are, the declaration explained, numerous disappearances even in a classic war, when the contenders are of different nationalities, uniforms are worn that differentiate between the two sides, and they are separated by perfectly identifiable lines. In a war as peculiar as Argentina's, in which the enemy did not wear a uniform and his identity papers were forged, the number of unidentified dead increases significantly.

This intentional inversion of the terms (the families were demanding information on the fate of identified people who had been taken alive, and the junta was answering them with unidentified dead bodies) introduced the report's central paragraph. In that paragraph, the junta denied the existence of secret detention centers and declared that the disappeared who were not living in exile or in hiding were dead, "even though up until now the cause and occasion of their death cannot be specified nor the location of their graves." As was customary in the military prose of that period, the report expressed the wish that the enemy dead would receive God's forgiveness.

The document did not reveal precisely what happened between the time of arrest of living persons—who had first names and family names, which the military forced them to reveal under torture—and their transformation into the anonymous dead whose corpses were floating in limbo. Eighty percent of the disappeared had been kidnapped in front of witnesses from their homes, from the street, or from their workplaces. It was a war without battles.

The document concluded by stating that only the judgment of history could determine with any exactitude who was responsible for unjust methods or innocent deaths, that the armed forces felt true Christian pain and recognized the "mistakes that may have been made" in fulfillment of their assigned mission. Here once again was the idea of a noble mission carried out, in which, at most, hypothetical mistakes of an unspecified nature could be conceded, subject to no review other than that of heaven or history.

With the presidential elections of 1983 one month away, the last military government signed the law of autoamnesty. Its initial clauses affirmed that the terrorism of the subversives had dictated the cruel and cunning form of the battle, which may have given rise over the course of the struggle to actions incompatible with the goals of the armed forces, which were fighting on the side of human dignity.

The pardon extended to all members of the military and their civilian collaborators who, still in hypothetical terms, "may have resorted to the use of procedures that went beyond the legal framework," not of their own will, naturally, but because of the aforementioned "imposition of unusual and extreme conditions under which those actions took place."

At that point, Scilingo was an aide to the chief of the Military House of the Presidency, Rear Admiral Ramón Arosa, who would become chief of staff of the navy under Alfonsín. "I think the list of the disappeared must be made public," Scilingo put to him in the days when the junta was publishing its "Final Document."

Arosa neither agreed nor disagreed.

The armed forces fled from the government on December 10, 1983, without ever having admitted to the aberrant acts that were committed under the orders of their leaders.

Chapter Seven
Boomerang

FROM THE first days of the dirty war, information about the fate of the disappeared prisoners began to flow, despite the strict censorship of the press and the military secrecy of the operations. With a little imprecision, information was even available about the flights, which Scilingo would describe in detail much later on.

On August 20, 1976, a cable from the Agency for Clandestine News (known as ANCLA, an acronym that, in Spanish, has the ironic naval meaning of "anchor"), created by the writer, journalist, and Montonero activist Rodolfo J. Walsh, stated that the government would never make the list of the prisoners known because "many of those listed had appeared as dead in combat on dates long after they were arrested." It cited the case of the Navy School of Mechanics, "where 160 prisoners appear on the books, out of whom only forty-five are actually being held there. None of the remaining prisoners has been sent to another prison, so it is believed that they have been eliminated and thrown into the Río de la Plata."

Shortly afterward, I wrote an extensive work on the Navy School of Mechanics entitled *History of the Dirty War in Argentina*, which ANCLA distributed both in and outside the country. It was the first systematic compilation of the diverse facts known about that clandestine concentration camp. It began:

September 6, 1976, marked the forty-sixth anniversary of the first twentieth-century military coup in Argentina. On that day, the handcuffed and mutilated corpses of three young men washed up from the Río de la Plata onto the Uruguayan coast.

That macabre spectacle has been repeated dozens of times since March 24, 1976, when the Argentine military took over the government once more and a military junta gave control to Army General Jorge Rafael Videla, the eleventh man to have moved from the barracks to the Pink House in Buenos Aires in the last half-century.

In November 1975, while still promising President María Estela Martínez (better known as Isabelita Perón) that he would obey the law, Videla participated in the XI Conference of American Armies, which took place on the initiative of the United States Pentagon. There he declared that, "In Argentina, there shall be as many deaths as are necessary for peace to reign again." The Conference of American Armies was held in Montevideo, the capital of Uruguay, where the military has governed for half a decade under a civilian mask.

Four months later, when Videla discarded that tactic for Argentina and took over the presidency from Mrs. Perón, the echo of his words was felt in Uruguay.

The first body was found a few days after the installation of the new Argentine military government. It was disfigured and difficult to identify. Officially, Uruguay reported that from the features it could be a Japanese or a Korean, and the Argentine press imagined a fantastical Asiatic orgy on the high seas that ended in tragedy.

The hypothesis prospered with the discovery of two more bodies, but it did not check out very well against the evidence. No ship cast adrift, no report of missing persons arrived to support it.

The river continued depositing its mysterious cargo on Uruguay's Atlantic beaches, which, with their fine sand and warm climate, are frequented by tourists from throughout the Southern Cone. Some corpses had been slashed, others had limbs missing, most did not have nails on their fingers or toes.

Uruguayan exiles in Paris reported that among the dead were four of their comrades who had been arrested by the Uruguayan government. The Uruguayan military authorities immediately called a press conference in Montevideo and brought the four supposed victims out to meet the journalists.

The dead bodies were neither Koreans nor Japanese nor Uruguayans. The government in Buenos Aires behaved as if it had nothing to do with the matter. Its greatest concern at that time was to reconcile the various factions that comprised it.

Further on, the report described the procedures adopted by the leaders of the military coup:

Small task forces wearing civilian clothing and driving unmarked vehicles secretly ambush their enemies and transport them to military buildings without giving official notice of their arrest. The Fight Against Subversion Order of Operations, given by the army high command in November 1975, indicated that "special interrogational methods" were to be applied in order to carry out a prolonged intelligence action. In other words, torture was to be used in order to gain access to information so as to carry out further covert operations.

The chapter on ESMA said that its offensive structure "consisted of the so-called 3.3 Task Force" and described its special operations: "some in uniform, others in civilian clothing, in unmarked vehicles with the support of divisions 30 and 45 of the Federal Police." The uniformed patrols went out two or three times a day in green trucks preceded by a patrol car. "On the other hand, the patrols in civilian clothing were not regularly spaced and were carried out on the basis of pieces of intelligence that had been previously obtained. Conscripted soldiers did not participate in them and they were led by officers, noncommissioned officers, and petty officers." The report included the model, color and license plate numbers of ten of the unmarked vehicles that were used in the kidnappings.

Under the subtitle "Cruel and Unusual Punishments," the testimony of a person imprisoned in the ESMA for three weeks appeared in the report:

> When, with a hood over my head, I arrived at the place where I would be held, I heard the sound of airplanes. To reach the building where I was kept, we crossed a very large room where very loud rock music was heard. I recognized it days later when they took me there to torture me. From that large room we entered an elevator, and after leaving it I was taken up a flight of nine stairs. I was placed in a room with other people whom I did not know, about twenty or thirty of them. All of them had their feet tied down with chains attached to shackles around their ankles. Most of the chains were also attached to columns or to very heavy pieces of iron. I had a hood over my head and my hands cuffed behind my back for the entire three weeks I was there. They did not remove the hood even for meals, but they did switch the handcuffs to the front so I could feed myself with my hands. We were guarded by men who, from their age, did not appear to be conscripted soldiers. We could only see their ankle boots through the lower part of the hood. If we tried to speak among ourselves we were beaten. One day they took me to the large room with modern music and then to a smaller room inside it. They used the electric cattle prod on me there.

"The electric cattle prod," the report explained:

> has a metal tip connected to two electrical poles which produce a charge upon contact with the skin. It is an Argentine invention. For a long time, rudimentary cattle prods were used in the stockyards to force the cattle in the direction desired by the horseman who was herding them to the corrals where they would be slaughtered. Similarly ingenious devices running on tiny batteries are still used today by jockeys who want to stimulate their mounts without running the risk of doping them, which leaves chemical traces.
>
> In the 1930s, during Argentina's first twentieth-century military dictatorship, the police began to use the electric cattle

prod to force confessions from presumed criminals. The cattle prod is a useful instrument of torture for avoiding evidence and the penalties that can befall torturers under a liberal regime in which judges, lawmakers, and journalists are watching to insure that any excesses are not scandalous; if the prod has been skillfully wielded, no marks are left on the skin a few days later.

But in today's Argentina, marks on the skin, judges, lawmakers, and journalists have all ceased to worry the military, which does not feel obliged to give an account of its actions to anyone and even allows itself to divulge, in brief communications, that a prisoner has died from cardiac arrest, without giving further details. The memories of the few prisoners who have succeeded in leaving the Navy School of Mechanics alive, freed when their lack of connection with the causes for which they were arrested was proven—or, in one case, having escaped—allow an approximate reconstruction of the range of cruel and unusual punishments employed there: the rape of women, the introduction of live mice into their vaginas, the mutilation of genitals with razor blades, vivisection without anesthesia, the amputation of limbs, the pulling off of finger- and toenails. The torture concludes with the death of the prisoners, who are thrown into the Río de la Plata or, when possible, transported in a navy ship to the high seas. For that reason, one of the corpses found in Uruguay had Argentine cigarettes, matches, and coins in its pants pockets.

This report identified eighteen victims and more than thirty of their torturers, among them the army officers Adolfo M. Arduino, Jorge Acosta, and Antonio Pernías, whose last name appeared without the final s. It also reprinted an open letter written by the former vice minister of education, Emilio Fermín Mignone, whose daughter Mónica had been abducted along with two priests and several catechism teachers in May 1976. Despite the denial of the naval commanders, Mignone pointed with certainty at the Navy School of Mechanics:

> Wasn't it denied, despite all the evidence, that the Jesuit priests Yorio and Jalics—who have been held incommunicado for three months without being charged with any-

thing—had been arrested? And the same thing happened with the fifteen catechists who were released with hoods over their heads and in chains after twelve hours of hunger and cold. The forces that took action on Sunday, May 23, at noon, in Bajo Flores quarter, said they were from the army and asked for support from the local police headquarters. Admiral Montes, chief of naval operations, who denies that my daughter is being held prisoner by his branch of the military (a statement I permit myself to doubt entirely), told me that the procedure had been carried out by the marine infantry, and that the kidnapped persons were taken to the Navy School of Mechanics. But all that was denied for two months, until the information was leaked by an officer's wife.*

The report reprinted extensive passages of Mignone's letter, which addressed the most essential aspects of the matter with a precision rare for a contemporary and even more rare in one who was a victim of the actions he discusses:

> Either those thousands of prisoners arrested by men of the armed forces on active duty are under your jurisdiction and in that case the military hierarchy is lying and putting on a huge farce when they receive us with smiles and kindness, or the officers who are acting in this way are not subordinate to your orders, in which case the situation is extremely grave.
>
> I ask that you calculate the consequences and the historical responsibility of those who rose to power under the banner of a state monopoly on power and a few months later cannot control even a noncommissioned officer. The dilemma is enormous, and if you are lying it is equally enormous because a state cannot be based on lies. I have explained all of this without receiving a satisfactory response in every one of the bureaus of the armed forces which the disappearance of my poor, good daughter has forced me to enter.

---

* Mónica Mignone and her friend Mónica Quinteiro, who had until recently been a nun, had been abducted together. One of Mónica Quinteiro's first cousins was the wife of the concentration camp's chief of intelligence, Commander Jorge Acosta, and one of Quinteiro's sisters was married to the man who, eighteen years later, as Admiral Molina Pico, would become the chief of staff of the navy. It seems likely that the cousin or the sister was the source Mignone mentions.

Mignone stated his view that the military authorities were practicing a "dirty war without seeing that it is suicide, in addition to being immoral. How can they not be aware that two years from now, if they have killed the twenty or thirty thousand marginal figures that they have taken prisoner or that they hope to take prisoner, or even if they release them after months in hiding, chained, hooded, and tortured, the literature on the subject is going to inundate the country and will turn like an unstoppable boomerang against the armed forces themselves?"

The report continued, "Another high functionary of a former military government,"

> Air Force General Jorge Landaburu, underwent the same agony as Mignone after the disappearance of one of Landaburu's daughters, who was twenty-three years old and a member of the Peronist University Youth.
>
> When she was captured by a squad from the Navy School of Mechanics, the young woman was in possession of another female prisoner's narrative of the tortures that were used on her before she had managed to escape from the school a few days earlier. For 150 days, this general was negotiating at the highest political and military levels, but the navy denied they were holding his daughter. At the end of September, nevertheless, officers of the school gave him his daughter's body; after five months of torture, she had been shot.
>
> It is difficult to estimate the number of victims, but it is known that between a basement that is very close to the runways of the Buenos Aires airport—almost all the narratives coincide in mentioning the intense noise of airplane engines—and an attic in the officers' building at the school, there are on a permanent basis about sixty prisoners, whose numbers are constantly being replenished. Some arrive, while others are thrown into the sea. About twenty-five corpses have already appeared in Uruguay, but out of all those who have been killed, this is believed to be only a small percentage, which because of technical errors slipped past the control of the authorities at the school and became known to the public.

In a special dispatch for the first anniversary of the military dictatorship, the ANCLA news agency distributed a cable on the human rights situation. One of its paragraphs reviewed the appearance of corpses in the Atlantic Ocean: "During a social gathering at the Mau Mau night club, a minister in the nation's cabinet boasted that 'now things are really going well because we put all the subversives in body bags, take them out on boats, and throw them into the sea: it's what we should have been doing from the beginning.' Responsible sources indicate that those murdered in this way number in the hundreds."

On March 24, 1977, in his "Open Letter from a Writer to the Military Junta," praised by Gabriel García Márquez as a masterpiece of universal journalism, Rodolfo J. Walsh wrote,

> Between fifteen hundred and three thousand people have been secretly massacred since you forbade the publication of information about the discovery of corpses, which in certain cases has come out nevertheless because it has affected other countries, because of its genocidal magnitude, or because of the fear provoked among your own forces. Twenty-five mutilated bodies washed up on the Uruguayan coast between March and October of 1976, a small part, perhaps, of the number of those tortured to death in the Navy School of Mechanics.
>
> Walsh rejected "the fiction of right-wing gangs," supposedly descended from the '3-A' groups (death squads) of José López Rega, the former minister under Isabelita (Perón), and capable of crossing the largest garrison in the country in military trucks, carpeting the Río de la Plata with dead bodies or throwing prisoners into the sea from the aircraft of the first air brigade without either General Videla, Admiral Massera, or Brigadier General Agosti becoming aware of it. Today, the 3-A are the 3-Armed Forces, and the junta you men preside over is not the needle on the scale between 'two opposing violent factions' nor the just arbitrator between 'two terrorisms' but the very source of terror that has lost its way and can only stammer out the discourse of death.

The next day, Walsh was ambushed by a squad from ESMA at an appointment one of his comrades had revealed to them under torture. Astiz was supposed to deliver him alive to the torture chambers. Walsh ruined his plan by grabbing the tiny .22-caliber

Walther PPK pistol he was hiding. It was useless for breaking through the circle of fifteen gunbarrels, but very eloquently expressed his will not to let them touch him. Before falling, he wounded the leg of a policeman who was later decorated for having been lamed in the line of duty. Five prisoners knew about the preparations for the operation, and one of them saw Walsh's body, riddled with bullet holes, at the Navy School of Mechanics. He believes they set it on fire, as Scilingo describes, on the athletic field, next to the river that figured in Walsh's final story.

Chapter Eight
Disinfection

IN THE Senate, Pernías admitted that the navy had participated in the abduction, torture, and disappearance of the French nuns Alice Domon and Leonie Duquet, but denied having taken part in it personally. He said that in the first series of accusations brought in France in 1979 or 1980 "I was not implicated at all in the matter." Only years later, "I began to be incriminated, but in a vague way, in the issue of the nuns."

The testimony that the survivors Sara Solarz de Osatinsky, Ana María Martí, and María Alicia Milia de Pirles gave in a chamber of the French National Assembly on October 12, 1979, refutes Pernías's claim. The text of that testimony affirms that the officers who participated in the operation against the nuns were Lieutenants Junior Grade Alfredo Aztis (*sic*) and Alfredo González Menotti, Lieutenants Schelling and Antonio Pernía (*sic*), Lieutenant Junior Grade Radizzi (*sic*) and the coast guard man Favre. The inexact spelling of the names resulted from the

limited information available at that time. "They were savagely
tortured. The conduct of both nuns was admirable. Even in the
worst moments of pain, Sister Alice, who was in Capucha,*
asked how her comrades were. Ironically, she asked in particular
about the 'little blond boy' who was none other than the navy
officer who had infiltrated the group, Lieutenant Junior Grade
Astiz." The prisoners at ESMA heard the officers calling them
the flying nuns. In 1979, a Spanish magazine reprinted part of
the survivors' declaration, illustrated with photographs of
Pernías and Rolón.

Even before that, in April 1978, the Argentine Commission
for Human Rights, which gathered the testimony of survivors in
exile, had published the narrative of Horacio Domingo Maggio,
a trade unionist who escaped from ESMA. Maggio told of his
dialogues with the nuns in the clandestine concentration camp.
"They were not wearing their habits and were very battered and
weak, because two guards had to take Sister Alice to the bathroom since she couldn't stand up." She told him that they had
tied her to a bed, completely naked, and passed the electric cattle
prod across her body. "They were at ESMA for approximately
eleven days, on most of which they were interrogated and
tortured. Then they were transferred along with eleven other
people, I don't know where." In a magazine published by
Uruguayan exiles in Sweden, Maggio identified Pernías among
the torturers of the nuns. There are no doubts about the chronol-
ogy here, because Maggio was killed a few months later.

One detail that continues to obsess the survivors was that
Astiz kissed the ones who were to be abducted, in order to identify them to their captors, who were watching from a distance.
The notice with the partial list of the disappeared was published
in the newspapers on Christmas Day 1977, and among the

---

* Capucha (hood) and Capuchita (little hood) were the names of the two rooms at
ESMA where the prisoners were held.

signatures appearing with it was that of Gustavo Niño, the name under which Astiz had pretended to be the brother of a disappeared man. During the trial of the former military leaders, the prosecution called as a witness the real Gustavo Niño, a thin, dark-skinned man who does not resemble the blond, rotund Astiz in the least.

Sara Solarz de Osatinsky, Ana María Martí, and María Alicia Milia de Pirles were set free by the 3.3 Task Force, which considered them "recuperated," to use the expression favored at ESMA. In their testimony, they also spoke of the method used to eliminate the prisoners, about which by then much more was known than during the first denunciations in 1976 and 1977. Their statement gives an idea of the feelings that the flights described by Scilingo aroused in the victims:

> On Wednesdays, or sometimes on Thursdays, transports took place. At first they told us that the captives were being taken to other prisons or to the work camps they said they had near the Rawson penitentiary in Patagonia. It was hard for us to convince ourselves that in reality the transport took them to their deaths. The day of the transport the atmosphere was very tense. We captives didn't know if we were going to be chosen that day or not. The guards were much more severe. We couldn't go to the bathroom. Each one of us had to stay rigidly in his place, with the hood and shackles on, without making any movements that might enable us to see what was going on. All of this happened in Capucha and Capuchita. The basement was completely evacuated around 3:30 P.M. If any captive was being tortured there, they took him up to the third floor. At around 4:00 P.M., in Capucha, they began calling up prisoners by their case numbers. They were formed into a single file line, holding onto each other's shoulders, since they were still wearing hoods and shackles. They led them down one by one. We could hear the noise the shackles made as they walked toward the door, which was opened and then immediately closed again. Each one took with him only the clothing he was wearing.
>
> They were taken to the infirmary in the basement, where the nurse would give them an injection to knock them out without killing them. In that state, still alive, they were taken

out the side door of the basement and put on a truck. Half-unconscious they were driven to the military airport, placed on board an airplane that flew south, out to sea, where they were thrown out alive. Often during the transport, helicopters could be heard flying over the area. For that reason we thought that sometimes the transports were carried out by that means. These statements are based on events we lived through during the two years spent in the officer's club at ESMA.

We never heard anything more about the thousands of prisoners who left on those collective transports. In a little room, the storeroom where the clothing the prisoners wore was kept, we often found the clothing our comrades had been wearing the day of the transport.

While preparations for the transport were being made, our regular guards didn't enter the basement either, but sometimes they had to, and when they came back to the third floor they were visibly upset. It was clear that they didn't fully understand what was going on. They said in an uncontrolled way that terrible things were happening in the basement, that the prisoners to be transported were dead or knocked out by an injection. During the transport operation only the nurse, two guards, the officer on duty, and his aide went into the basement. The nurse went there hours before the transport with a box full of bottles and syringes.

One of the guards who was nicknamed "Bolita" (a derogative term for Bolivian immigrants) was present during almost all the transports, even on the days he was supposed to have off. Another who was always present was the one we called "la Bruja" (the Witch). Once he was seen coming back after a transport in a navy truck with a green canvas canopy in back; he took from the truck a long metal box full of shackles, which he carried down to the basement. We received a little information about the transports from the officers, too. It escaped them in moments of weakness. The coast guard officer Gonzalo Sánchez, a.k.a. "Chispa" (Sparkle), said that the bodies were thrown into the sea in the south, in areas close to naval stations.

At first Captain Acosta forbade any reference to the subject of the transports. In moments of hysteria, he made statements such as: "Here any troublemaker gets a shot of penthonaval and goes up." The suffix -naval added to the name of a medicine is a common form of speech in the navy. The expression "goes up" means "gets killed." Acosta also confirmed that of all the prisoners who passed through there, the only ones left alive would be those in the group that the navy would later liberate. All the others would die. According to him, the hand of God would be present in this selection.

At the end of February 1977, there was a case of a mistaken transport, when our companion Tincho came back to Capucha. Tincho was physically very strong and was active in the Peronist Montonero movement. He was arrested in January. He had been a noncommissioned artillery officer in the navy. At the end of February, the guards called him up for transport. They took him down to the infirmary in the basement, where he was told he was going to be taken to a place where the conditions were better, but that he would first receive a vaccination to protect him from becoming infected with anything. The nurse gave him an injection in the arm, which took some time to have any effect. After a few minutes, Tincho began to feel that his arms and legs were no longer responding and that he was moving them as if in slow motion. He felt very weak, but did not fall asleep. The other prisoners felt the same. Some of them vomited while they were seated on the benches along the hallway in the basement. In some transports, there were a few who passed out, and they were dragged outside.

Tincho was taken out by the basement door and put in a truck which took him to the military airport. They started to put him on board a Fokker airplane. From above, Bolita asked his name. When he answered that he was Tincho, Bolita said, "You just saved yourself, kid," and took him back to ESMA. He was put back in Capucha. Tincho slept all that night and the following day. He was taken away in an individual transport a few days later. Afterward we learned that in mid-1977 he was being held captive in a prison controlled by the army. We don't know what happened to him.

Another similar case occurred at the end of August 1977. On a day when there weren't usually transports, they cleared out the basement and took down three male prisoners who had been in Capuchita. That same night they brought them back up unconscious and covered in vomit. Bolita and several guards brought them. One of the guards was the one they called "el abuelo" (Grandpa). Two female prisoners who were coming out of the bathroom saw two of the prisoners thrown down onto a thick beige canvas that was in front of the doorway leading into Capuchita. The third one was being taken up by Bolita and the guards, who were complaining because something had gone wrong with the transport. Two or three days later, those prisoners were taken away again and they never reappeared.

We weren't allowed to enter the basement until the day after the transport, even if it finished early. The next day the basement looked cleaner than usual, with the smell of disinfectant. Sometimes on the day of a transport we were told we had to clear out of the basement because it was going to be disinfected. Several times, they referred to the transport as "disinfection." Although the thorough cleaning was clearly intended to erase any possible evidence of what had happened the day before, there were many times when it was done quite negligently and we could see the marks of the bodies that were dragged from the infirmary to the side door of the basement. The most noticeable marks were the ones left by shoes or sneakers with rubber soles. In the hours following the transport, our anguish became even greater. On the one hand, we had another week of life ahead of us, but on the other hand we could see from the mattresses that were left empty which of our comrades had been taken away. And then we wept for them again, between pain, powerlessness, and rage. From what we were able to learn, ESMA was designated from the beginning as a place where prisoners were to be assembled, in other words where the prisoners were concentrated for subsequent transport.

The following organizational diagram was seen by a prisoner held by the navy:

Dump
Dump   Center for concentration   Hospital
Dump   of prisoners

From this diagram we were able to deduce that the final destination had been designated by the term "hospital."

The testimony of Lila Pastoriza, who was captured by the navy in 1977 and freed in 1978, coincides with this:

During the times when the repressive activity was at its height, the collective transports took place on a weekly basis, according to the guards and prisoners. The number of those transported varied each time: in some cases the transports included as many as forty or fifty prisoners. Individual transports could take place on any day at any hour. In general, the guard on duty would summon the prisoners and take them away with him. There was neither the strictness nor the display of repression that was made during the mass transports.

The first transport I was present for took place on June 16 or 17, 1977. Since I was being held in the basement, I was led to Capucha completely blindfolded, and there I heard approximately fifty numbers called out, corresponding to the prisoners. Later I learned that it was one of the last transports to be so numerous.

During my time in Capuchita I believed—though without much conviction—the explanations for the transports that the members of the repressive groups gave out: the prisoners were taken to another place (to farms and detention centers in the south, they said) until the question of what to do with them was resolved, or in fulfillment of a sentence that supposedly had been given to them. The only indicator that supported that possibility was the knowledge that one or another transported prisoner had been seen (individually) in another place. About the rest of them, I never learned anything. From conversations with the officers, I became convinced that the objective of the repressive action was the physical extermination of the prisoners. Although I never had any direct indication of what happened during the transports, other prisoners did. The hypothesis that one of the destinations of the prisoners was to be thrown into the sea from airplanes emerged from actions that were observed, fragmentary conversations with officers, stories told by the guards about a prisoner who was taken away by mistake and brought back from the airport. But it was always a taboo subject and any attempt at verification was forbidden. It was known among us that the list of those to be transported was drawn up in a meeting of intelligence officers (in the case of ESMA) which took place the day before. Also, a record of each captive was prepared, which was kept in the intelligence archives. At least after the date of my capture, everyone who arrived as a prisoner at ESMA was photographed and assigned a case number and an identifying record was prepared (sometimes including a test of political attitudes), which, according to the naval officers, was given to the First Corps of the army.

It seemed impossible to go on denying these facts. But eleven more years went by before Scilingo would tell the truth.

Chapter Nine
A Humanist in Uniform

IN 1983, the newly sworn-in president, Raúl Alfonsín, asked Congress to repeal the military's autoamnesty and asked the courts to prosecute the first three military juntas for homicide, unlawful deprivation of liberty, and application of torture to prisoners. He reformed the Code of Military Justice so that the rulings of the military courts could be appealed in the civil courts. All those who planned, organized, and controlled the operation of the machinery of repression, knowing it would produce extremely serious violations of human dignity, as well as those who took advantage of it for their personal benefit or with cruelty and perversity, were to be punished. But it was "imperative that those members of the armed forces and the law enforcement agencies who did not act on their own initiative when they participated in acts injurious to human dignity be offered the opportunity to serve the constitutional democracy loyally."

This last phrase was a first draft of Alfonsín's law of Due Obedience. But Congress established that there would be no possible excuse for "atrocious and aberrant actions"—such as torturing prisoners or throwing them out of airplanes alive into the sea.

The military courts ordered the rigorous preventive imprisonment of Massera and Videla. Massera was already in jail for the disappearance of Fernando Branca, the husband of one of his mistresses during a sailing party aboard the yacht Massera had use of as commander in chief of the navy.

Branca's goods were sold at a loss over the following months, thanks to documents bearing his authorization that were legalized by the Argentine consul in Miami, who died after carrying out the task. The notary who registered other sales and the overseer of one of Branca's operations also suddenly died of heart failure. The serial number of a telegram in which Branca had supposedly notified his administrator that he was leaving on a trip in fact corresponded to a cable containing congratulations on a marriage that was sent to a member of Massera's family.

The correspondent of the Spanish daily paper *El País,* José Luis Martín Prieto, wrote, "The transcript of the trial was dripping with blood, semen and tears, adultery, high class prostitution, passion, murder, forgeries, deceptions, plundering, corruption, arrogance. And what does all the sordidness of the case matter—it could be asked—next to the drama of military intervention and all the horrors of the Navy School of Mechanics? It matters, and matters a great deal. Until the Branca case, the members of the military who demolished their country in 1976 could retrospectively appear to be a group of misguided gentlemen who fell into the error of believing that the end, a good end, justified the means. After the Branca case, Admiral Massera and his comrades are seen in a new and more illustrative light: as men who, in the name of Christian civilization and the sacred principle of the Fatherland, were sleeping with a business partner's wife, then

killed the business partner and divided up his goods, as leftist rev-
olutionaries were screaming under torture in the prisons."

When Massera made his statement to the military court, he
said that during the dirty war the navy had jurisdiction only over
the sea, the rivers, their banks, and the port zones. When the general who was presiding over the tribunal asked him if he had ever
received any information regarding kidnappings, secret detention
centers, torture, assassinations, or violations of decency and sex-
ual freedom, Massera replied unhesitatingly: "At no time."

He added that every month he visited each unit and warned
those in command "to act with prudence because within two or
three years, or five or six or seven, as is happening now, yester-
day's heroes were going to become tomorrow's enemies. If there
have been excesses in anything, they must be isolated excesses
that will have to be analyzed." Massera passed the responsibility
off onto his subordinates: "It isn't because the admiral gives the
order that operations are carried out," he said, "it's because
those beneath want to carry them out." The general asked again,
"Did you have any knowledge of excesses that led to the execution of prisoners without any type of trial?"

"No, Mr. President," he answered.

Massera denied the very existence of the clandestine concentration camps. One of the members of the tribunal wanted to
know if there were any prisoners in places other than the designated ones such as jails or police stations.

"According to the information I have, no, sir. No person was
detained in any navy facility," he said.

He was also asked what meaning he gave to the term "annihilate." "A conceptual one, because the navy doesn't have an
operative dictionary where the term 'annihilate' is defined,"
Massera answered.

"The annihilation of subversion—did it justify the adoption
of extreme measures such as torture, illegal imprisonment,
homicide?" he was asked.

"Obviously not. None of the objectives of the process of national reorganization can justify what the president is referring to. On the contrary, the general conception of the process's activities was Western, humanist, Christian. I once pointed out that man should be the end of politics and not the target. In other words, man is the primordial thing. During the war against subversion, some mistakes may have been made. But if you ask me to mention one of them I cannot, because I reject the idea that excesses may have been committed; if any excesses were committed, within the sphere of the navy each time there was an awareness of something an investigation was carried out. Unfortunately, the tabloid press has mounted a campaign of slander and has made the population believe in some way in the unethical conduct of the armed forces, a notion which I spurn right now," said the leader who gave the order to use torture in interrogating prisoners.

"What were the limits placed on the freedom of action granted at the various operative levels?" the president of the tribunal wished to know.

"It could not exceed the limits of the lawful principles of warfare."

"Did you have any knowledge of the alleged irregularities that occurred within the navy's area of responsibility?"

"No, Mr. President. The information was very vague. The accusations that are being formulated are accusations woven together by prepared witnesses who are trying to fabricate a responsibility on the part of the armed forces. At that time there was no knowledge of any complaint about the supposed facts that are being alluded to today," Massera insisted.

Then he was queried about a Swedish teenager, 17-year-old Dagmar Hagelin, and the French nuns, all abducted by ESMA task forces. The two cases had extensive international repercussions because of the nationalities and identities of the victims. "I don't remember the issue of Sweden and France ever coming up.

I remember the events because they were in my time and of course an investigation was attempted within the capacity that the force had, without any positive result," he answered. He denied that there had ever existed an operative plan "based on manifestly illegal methods and procedures," and he "emphatically" rejected the idea that "thousands of people were illegally deprived of their freedom, tortured, and killed," and said that the Navy School of Mechanics had been chosen "as the particular target to be discredited. Fantastical and slanderous accusations emerged that I assert will never be proven because they are false." He added that "in the navy there do not exist nor have there ever existed public or secret regulations intended to safeguard procedures that are at variance with the principles of ethics."

Massera's successor at the navy, Admiral Armando Lambruschini, was also questioned by the military courts. "We are living in a time of great confusion in which the highest ethical values have been thrown into disarray. Let's suppose that a cancer has appeared, subversion, which seeks to disrupt the Argentine way of life and operations are undertaken to eradicate it. Over time, it turns out that the cancer was good and the eradication was bad," he said. He did not remember any details about the operations.

A few days later, the National Commission on the Disappeared delivered its final report. To the crimes of the terrorists, the report stated, the armed forces responded with an infinitely worse terrorism, bringing about the greatest and most savage tragedy of Argentine history, which attained the shadowy category of crimes against humanity. With the technique of disappearance and its consequences, all the ethical principles of the great religions and the most lofty philosophies erected over thousands of years of suffering and disaster were trampled on and barbarically ignored, it said.

These words caused a commotion in the country and stupefaction in the barracks. At that point, the government and a good part of the population had only recently become aware of the breadth and depth of the horror that for so many years had been denounced only by its victims and various human rights organizations.

The enormous documentation assembled by the National Commission on the Disappeared proved that human rights had been violated in an institutional and nationwide manner, with similar kidnappings and identical tortures throughout the country—which destroyed the theory of individual excesses. With particular passion, the commission described the situation of the disappeared person: from the moment of abduction, the victim lost all rights; he or she was cut off entirely from the outside world, imprisoned in unknown places, made to endure hellish torments, kept in ignorance of his near or immediate future, and subject to being thrown into the river or the sea with blocks of cement on his feet, or burned to ashes; and these were living creatures who maintained all the attributes of human beings: sensitivity to torture, the memory of their mothers, their children, their wives, shame at public violation—beings possessed by infinite anguish and supreme terror, but who kept a wild gleam of hope in some distant corner of their souls.

The commission certified that it had registered the cases of nearly nine thousand of these forsaken souls, but stated that it had every reason to suppose that the actual number was higher, because many families hesitated to file a complaint about the kidnappings for fear of reprisals.

A synthesis of the commission's report was published under the title *Nunca Más*. The English edition, also titled *Nunca Más* (New York: Farrar, Straus, & Giroux, 1986), reports on page 221, under the subtitle, "Prisoners thrown into the sea":

> This is scarcely credible, but is mentioned by many witnesses; some because they had heard about it, others because of direct references made by their captors. Then there were the bodies washed up by currents on the shore. It is indeed difficult to believe, but in the general context of this savage repression one can imagine that for those who practiced it, it was just one more method among many with the same purpose.

The commission linked the testimony of the survivors to a news article that appeared in 1983 about thirty-seven corpses that had been picked up on various beaches. "The sea, which has very irregular currents in the gulf region, washed them up onto the sand in an extremely disfigured condition. On some bodies, unmistakable signs of violence were observed: salt water and hungry fish had disfigured almost all of them. All of them came from the open sea. They may have fallen from a ship or have been thrown out of airplanes, in the opinion of an expert"—a decade before Scilingo's confession.

The day following the release of the commission's conclusions, the military tribunal notified the civil courts that it could not hand down a ruling within the allotted time and declared that "the decrees, directives, operational orders, etc., that governed the military activity against the terrorist subversion were, with respect to form and content, unobjectionable."

The tribunal also maintained that deprivation of freedom was not illegitimate in the case of persons who had broken the law and stated its belief that the prosecution was motivated by the complaints of persons who were implicated, or their family members, and whose objectivity and credibility were therefore relative. As the orders given were unobjectionable, the military council did not acknowledge any possible responsibility on the part of the former high command other than for their lack of control over the illicit deeds that their subordinates may have committed. Once again, the guilt lay with the lower ranks.

The civil courts took over the case that the military tribunal had no intention of proceeding with, and in April 1985, public hearings began in the trial of nine former commanders in chief of the armed forces, among them three former military presidents.

Chapter Ten
The Judgment of Mankind

THE MEMBERS of the military juntas who had made the entire society tremble until just a few years before rose respectfully to their feet on the order of a young clerk each time the members of the federal chamber that was judging them returned to the courtroom. But all nine denied having ordered the use of methods that were injurious to human rights. They did not acknowledge the facts and accused the concentration camp survivors of fabricating their testimony about a descent into hell. They suggested that their judges, too, were part of a sinister conspiracy against the virtuous guardians of the nation. If any mistake had been made, it was the responsibility of their subordinates.

Victims and victimizers told their respective stories during the trial's public hearings, which went on throughout 1985.

Vice Admiral Luis María Mendía was in charge of naval operations and was responsible for formulating, writing, and carrying out the navy's plans, in fulfillment of the decrees of the

National Executive Power ordering that the activities of the subversive elements be annihilated.

Mendía said that according to the dictionary, "annihilate" means "destroy, reduce to nothing." He explained that "the armed forces are violent, destructive, they have no half-measures. We don't use tear gas. If gases are used, they're lethal gases." He cited Clausewitz's phrase on war and politics and said that according to the decrees of the Executive Power, adopted before the coup that overthrew the government of Isabel Perón, politics had exhausted its possibilities without overcoming the destructive effects of terrorism. "We were facing a war."

Mendía insisted that the navy had not acted in fragmented factions or in paramilitary form, but institutionally, in accordance with its permanent operative organization. He also denied that there had been clandestine or illegal detention centers. He said that suspects were summarily interrogated at naval facilities by intelligence officers. If their lack of connection with any subversive organization was proven, they were freed. If their participation in such groups was determined, they remained under detention "for the necessary and prudent time" and then passed into the hands of "the corresponding legal authority." Once it was established whether or not they were involved, "the corresponding process was initiated." "The appropriate steps" were taken.

"Was the clause of the plan according to which the detention would last no longer than forty-eight hours, in order for a declaration to be taken, complied with?"

"It was complied with insofar as possible. The standard procedure was to take the time that was necessary. Sometimes forty-eight hours was not enough."

"How did the intelligence personnel conduct the interrogations?"

"They were conducted in compliance with the regulations on interrogations."

"Do you remember those regulations?"

"In a natural, noncoercive way, calmly, and without pressure on the interrogated person."

Next, Vice Admiral Pedro Santamaría, the former top ranking officer of the coast guard, swore to tell the truth. He was asked if he recalled the appearance of corpses along the coast.

"Nothing out of the ordinary," answered the man who was responsible for the movements of the Skyvan planes.

The French Admiral Antoine Sanguinetti, who in 1977 had been part of an international delegation that investigated the disappearance of the nuns and another sixteen French citizens, also made a declaration. Massera had told the delegation, "I acknowledge that there are some groups in the army that are out of control. One could call them Fascists, if the term were not so unpleasant. I disapprove of this situation, for which I am not responsible. The navy and the air force have no responsibility." He invited them to visit a naval base to verify that there were no *desaparecidos* there.

The journalist Jacobo Timerman told the judges about a strange lunch in Buenos Aires's most luxurious hotel with one of Massera's closest collaborators, Captain Carlos Bonino, shortly after the coup d'etat.

> He explained their theory of repression to me, in a kind and dispassionate tone. He said that it had to be irreversible, because that was the only way of eliminating subversion forever. Anyone who might be linked to subversion, whether they were children, parents, or relatives, had to disappear. It was a sacrifice Argentina had to make and it would be worth it.
>
> "It would be better to declare martial law and use the death penalty, but with the opportunity to mount a defense in front of a tribunal," I argued with him.
>
> "We're in a hurry. We don't have time. In a situation like that, the pope would intervene, and it would be very difficult to send people to the firing squad against the pope's wishes," he answered me.
>
> "But Franco sent people to the firing squad against the pope's opposition," I insisted.
>
> "We're not in a position to do that," he replied.

Timerman added that during the same lunch, an executive of the Italian multinational Olivetti had asked about the man who was responsible for an attempt at poisoning the food of naval officers. Bonino answered him, without any change of tone: "We threw him into the ocean."

In the months that elapsed between the March 1976 coup and his own abduction in April 1977, Timerman, who was then the editor of the daily paper *La Opinión,* also met with Massera. "I tried to convince him of the necessity of exerting repression within a legal framework. 'Don't worry about that. Go on a vacation—everything will work out. This isn't a world in which we can acknowledge what we're doing, but it's going to end quickly,' he answered."

The prosecutor, Julio Strassera, asked Timerman to say more about the international pressure Massera said was keeping them from exerting repression within a legal structure. Timerman responded: "He said what all the navy men said, that against the pope's protests it's impossible to send people to the firing squad. He told me that the country's international credit, managed by the minister of economic affairs, would be affected," Timerman answered.

Marta Bettini de Devoto testified that she had never again heard from her husband, Lieutenant Junior Grade Jorge Devoto, after the day he went to the headquarters of the commander in chief of the navy to ask about a man who had disappeared.

"Did your husband hear comments from his colleagues about how the repression was being carried out?" she was asked.

"A lot. I myself heard that they were throwing people into the sea from navy planes and that some of them were troubled by their consciences."

The Catholic priests Orlando Yorio and Francisco Jalics were kidnapped in May 1976 and taken to ESMA, where they were asked about their friend, the former nun Mónica Quinteiro. After five months of captivity, "They gave us an injection. They said it was a vaccine. We were very dizzy, and they put us in a truck. It stopped, they gave us another injection, and moved us to another vehicle, which had a grooved floor. In that vehicle, they gave us a third injection and I lost consciousness," Yorio said.

But the priests lived to tell the tale. "When I came to," Yorio testified, "I was lying on fresh grass, blindfolded but otherwise unshackled. We were like drunks, in the middle of the country-side, in the dark, surrounded by swamps. A farmer told us that the previous afternoon he had seen a helicopter landing. There wasn't any other way to get there."

The same day Yorio spoke, Captain Oscar Quinteiro, then sev-enty-three years old, whose daughter Mónica was abducted as she left her job at a military life insurance company, told the court about his nightmare. Quinteiro paid a visit to the president of the company, an army general, who showed him the employee time chart for that day: his daughter had left the office in normal fash-ion. His peregrination continued to the ministry of the interior, where General Albano Harguindeguy informed him that Mónica did not figure on any register of prisoners. By means that he did not reveal, Quinteiro learned that his daughter was at the Navy School of Mechanics, but the school's assistant director, Salvio Menéndez, also denied that. "From the way he answered, I realized he wasn't telling the truth," Quinteiro testified. "Since I insisted, he went into another room. He said he was going to see if her name appeared. When he returned, he repeated that she did not appear on any list. I thanked him and left him my telephone number." The only person who called him was the general from the insurance company to say that if Mónica did not reappear within three days he would put her on notice with a certified telegram and in another ten days she would be fired. But since she was a good employee, she could have her job back if she reappeared.

Quinteiro met six times with his former student Emilio Massera. The first time he asked for Massera's authorization to present an appeal for habeas corpus to the courts.

"No, Captain. I will see to this personally and will keep you informed," Massera answered.

His daughter's fellow workers told him that she had been arrested as she left the office. For the second time, Quinteiro went back to see the director of the company where she had worked.

"Look, Captain, I take good care of the personnel. If someone had come, you would be the first person I would have told," the man repeated.

Months later, Quinteiro reprehended the company's assistant director, a vice commodore of the air force.

"You know and you must tell me."

"A major and two policemen came to get her. Since the director was busy, they were sent to my office. I was opposed to their arresting her there and suggested to them that I have someone call her so that they could recognize her," the vice commodore admitted.

Quinteiro could hardly go on with his story. "The assistant director asked an employee to call my daughter and had her taken to an office with glass walls and curtains. Through the glass walls, those men saw my daughter. I would like you to put yourselves in my place when I learned this, so much later, and told by the man who did it himself, when the director had sworn to me that it hadn't happened. Sad and indignant, I went directly to the commander in chief of the navy and told him that I was going to file a lawsuit."

"Wait, first I'm going to talk to the vice commodore," Massera said, cutting him off.

The vice commodore said he would not be able to identify the men who kidnapped Mónica. Only then did Massera give Quinteiro permission to undertake judicial action, which as usual had no results.

In one of their conversations, Massera told Quinteiro that neither the army nor the navy was holding his daughter, and that it only remained to check with the air force. "Admiral, many officers are lying to you," the despairing father answered, still trusting his colleague's sincerity.

"Did you come to any conclusions about which branch of the military arrested your daughter and what her fate was?" the court asked him.

"From what the priest Orlando Yorio told me, I have no doubt that she was at ESMA and that the commander in chief of the navy was perfectly aware not only of what was going on with my daughter but of everything that was happening in his force. The day of the national holiday, Yorio heard a speech that ended with the ritual salute, 'School of Mechanics, subordination, and courage' and the response 'To serve the fatherland.' In the basement where he was being held, he heard someone say, 'Ay, Orlando,' and recognized my daughter's voice."

"What did Massera say when you told him they were lying to him?" the prosecutor asked.

"He didn't give any answer at all."

The tribunal asked Alejandro Hugo López, a conscripted soldier who had once worked at ESMA, "Did you hear anything about the fate of the prisoners?"

"Yes. In the construction storeroom I saw a tub that was six feet long and a foot high, with a grill on top. On one side was a tube with an upright funnel. They put the bodies in there and added gasoline through the funnel. That's how they would disappear," he answered.

Then he added, "There were two ways of disappearing: flight or grill."

The former ESMA cadet Jorge Carlos Torres recalled for the tribunal that, "The noncommissioned officer told us they were going to burn a body. Beyond the athletic field, fires could often be seen."

Retired Commander Jorge Félix Búsico, a former director of studies at ESMA, said that every day he saw columns of vehicles coming in with hooded prisoners but he never saw them leaving. Twice he heard screams of pain.

"Did you ever see instruments of torture?"

"I didn't see them, but people were talking about a device that was used. It was hard for me to accept. I had no desire to know. I resisted accepting that naval officers would do that."

"Was anyone killed?" he was asked.

"A whole jargon appeared: suck in (*chupar*; for abductions), wall in (tabicar; for blindfolding), send up (*mandar para arriba*), which meant execution. It was commonly used in ESMA when someone died, unfortunately. I saw helicopters operating in the parade square, which is the nerve center of the school, and in less visible places."

Búsico was removed from the task forces for having questioned the use of false names.

"What did the director and assistant director of ESMA say when they reprimanded you for identifying yourself in front of the prisoners?" a judge asked him.

"That these were covert operations and all the officers had to conceal their names."

"Did they give any reasons why?"

"At my insistence, Admiral Chamorro said that it was a matter of confusing the enemy. They shouldn't know if their comrades had been captured or had left the country, either. This would undermine their morale."

"What was your reply to that?"

"That it didn't seem right to me and that I doubted whether these methods were militarily apt, since they had ended in disaster in other places in the world where they were used. The whole thing frightened me a great deal. When I worked up the nerve to bring the matter up again, I saw that it was rigidly decided on."

"Did you know any other dissidents?"

"Among the officers who weren't affected by the fight against subversion the subject was avoided, but human life had no value, it didn't matter whose it was. There was a refusal to speak. It was difficult for an officer to bring up his disagreement very often."

"And at the other places where you were stationed?"

"The same as at ESMA. Those who were not participating felt dissociated from it. That is not my case; I felt like an accomplice."

"Why do you say 'accomplice?'"

"Because I collaborated with my silence. I didn't have the courage to denounce it."

His career ended abruptly. At the end of 1977, he was informed that because he had gotten a divorce he would not be selected for command duties, despite having been congratulated for having reorganized and placed on a wartime footing the communication system of the Argentine navy's only aircraft carrier, of which he was second in command.

Rosario Evangelina Quiroga was arrested in Montevideo, the capital of neighboring Uruguay, transported in secret to Buenos Aires, and held at ESMA. "The hallway leading to the torture chambers was identified by a sign that said 'Avenue of Happiness,'" Quiroga testified to the court. "When they were torturing, they would play a record at high volume to hide the screams. In one of the torture chambers there was a cross on the wall, which was said to have been drawn by one of the French nuns." She added that those "about whose subsequent fate we had no knowledge whatsoever," were called "the transported ones . . . because they didn't come back to the school. All the naval officers that served at or attended ESMA and frequented the officers' club had contact with the prisoners, or knew about their presence in that establishment, because it was inevitable that they saw them shackled or handcuffed and hooded." The prisoners could be freed, as happened to her, or "be transported to another clandestine detention camp; or be eliminated." A priest in the military vicar's office obtained a

Venezuelan visa for her at the request of her captors, and Rolón took her to the Ezeiza airport.

Graciela Daleo told the court that the day she was arrested she was led to ESMA's torture room number 13. Pernías warned her: "You're in our hands. If you don't talk, you're going up. You're going to tell us who your comrades are." While they applied electric charges to her body, she "screamed out Ave Marias and that enraged him. Pernías had a crucifix and a medal of the miraculous Virgin around his neck." Afterward "They put me in a car. After making a few turns, which I believe were within ESMA itself, they took me out. Pernías informed me that because I refused to give away my comrades they had decided to shoot me. There was one shot and then someone said: 'What lousy aim.'

"They touched my jacket. One of them said: 'Take it off her, I want it for my wife.'

"There were three more shots. Then they made me kneel, they put a gun to my temple, and they fired off another shot into the air." She added that one day Captain Acosta, the leader of the task force, told her: "I talk with baby Jesus every day. If he says you have to die, I give you a penthonaval and you go up."

According to Miriam Lewin, another survivor, "From stories told by the guards and some prisoners, it was known that (the transported prisoners) received an injection of penthonaval in the basement, they were loaded onto trucks, and rumor had it that they were then thrown into the sea from airplanes."

A small group of prisoners was selected for what the navy called a "recuperation process," led by Rolón. The former prisoner Andrés Castillo testified that he was able to identify Rolón when a group of prisoners were transported to a ranch on the outskirts of Buenos Aires. As they were going through a very well-known neighborhood, the navy man commented, "'All this belonged to my grandfather, but since he squandered his fortune there's only one avenue left.'

"'Your name is Rolón,' I told him.

"'How do you know?' he said, startled.

"'This is where two avenues, Fondo de la Legua (End of the Mile) and Rolón, begin. Your grandfather couldn't have been named End of the Mile.'

"He laughed and admitted I was right."

Like Penelope, Castillo wrote, on his captors' orders, a history of Argentine trade unionism which he then destroyed. Rolón "told me personal things. He had gone through a separation and then remarried. He brought me soccer magazines, and to keep me from being killed he said it would have disrupted the recuperation process of the seven other prisoners who were friends of mine. At Christmas, he brought me a loaf of fruit cake his sister-in-law had baked. He was a bit touched. I don't want to excuse him, but he did have a sense of guilt. He told me, 'I'm on duty and a bunch of prisoners came in. I can't take that machine (the electric cattle prod) any more.'"

The son of a naval officer who was obliged to retire because of personal conflicts with his superior officer and who was never able to adjust to civilian life, Rolón grew up with the mandate to fulfill his father's truncated career. While serving at the Navy School of Mechanics, he married a niece of the minister of economic affairs under the military dictator José Martínez de Hoz. His in-laws suggested that he ask for retirement and become the administrator of a family business, where he would earn five times more than in the navy and would not be in any danger. After thinking it over, Rolón rejected the offer. He believed that ESMA torture chambers were an unavoidable port of call on his voyage to an admiralship.

According to various testimonies, he was the officer who treated the prisoners best. One of them was about to be freed. A week before the announced date, Rolón entered his cell and showed him a newspaper. On the front page was a photograph of a member of the Shah of Iran's police force being chased by a group of women who were fighting to tear off his uniform. The prisoner gave the newspaper back without saying anything. In the concentration camp, it wasn't a good idea to say much.

"What do you think of that?" Rolón asked.

"What do I think of what?"

Rolón pointed to the photo. The prisoner picked up the newspaper again and confined himself to saying, "A Savak officer who's having some problems."

"Yes. But what do you think of it?"

"In what sense?" the prisoner, whose life depended on the navy man's mood, eluded the question again.

"Do you think it would be possible here?" Rolón asked.

The complex relationship between victims and victimizers did not allow for linear responses.

"If you're asking me if it's possible that a crowd could run after all of you in the street, I would say that I don't think so," the prisoner began. "If what you want to know is whether you will ever be asked to account for what you did, my opinion is that you will be."

"How we will be asked to account?" Rolón continued.

"I don't know. We've done a lot of stupid things, but you've committed atrocities and you'll have to explain them," the prisoner hazarded.

"You think there will be some kind of trial?"

"Yes."

Rolón asked the question the prisoner feared most: "If there were a trial, would you testify?"

The prisoner had no alternative. If he lied and Rolón realized he was lying, he would lose his confidence. If he told the truth, it might enrage Rolón.

"Yes," he answered.

"And what would you say?" Rolón asked.

"The truth."

"You'd say that I don't like torturing?"

"Yes, because it's the truth."

For an instant, there was a balance in the seesaw of power.

"Would you say that when I'm on intelligence duty I shut myself up in my room and turn off the light?"

"Yes."

"And that I don't answer when they call me, so they'll think I'm not there and someone else will interrogate the new prisoners?"

"I would say that, because it's the truth. But I would also talk about those you did torture," the prisoner concluded.

Rolón said nothing more and left the cell. A week later, together with a younger officer, Rolón drove the prisoner to the airport, where he flew off to freedom. The airplane flew over the highway on which Rolón and Astiz would return to the School of Mechanics. That prisoner would be one of the witnesses in the 1985 trial.

A former prisoner Carlos Muñoz informed the judges that at ESMA there was a file on each prisoner, which was microfilmed. It contained the prisoner's name, his number, his background, his story as he had written it at ESMA, the names of those who abducted him, the date, the political group he belonged to, and the sentence. *T* meant transport and *L* liberty. "In 1979, when the three women testified in Paris, I was ordered to look for their case files. There were five thousand cases in four boxes of microfilm, and there were very few *L*'s among them. That was where I got a sense of the dimensions of the slaughter," Muñoz said.

Against all this evidence, Massera denied everything once more in his personal statement before the judges. "Everyone knows that you don't transform officers and noncommissioned officers of the army, the air force and the navy into a gang of surprising assassins which from one day to the next loses all sense of ethics."

But it didn't happen from one day to the next. The former naval officer Julio César Urien, who later participated in

the Montonero guerrilla movement and spent the entire dictatorship period in prison, was sent in 1971 to ESMA, where
he took a course in antisubversive fighting. "The idea was
to involve everyone. We acted as paramilitary men, learning
to follow, abduct, and break someone," he told U.S. journalist
Tina Rosenberg.

"Break? How?"

"By torture."

During the course, Urien was assigned the role of the communist enemy leader. "We did exercises in which they really tortured me with electric charges, by hanging me from a bar
and with the submarine—putting my head under water. Then
they studied my reactions. They taught us that torture was
a moral way of fighting the enemy. In that way, they isolated
us from society. They brought in priests who said, 'Yes, that's
OK.' Some of the men had problems with learning to torture.
But the conditioning was that whoever didn't torture was
weak," he said.

With an actor's gestures, Massera recited a speech by someone else which he had memorized in prison: "I haven't come here
to defend myself. I've come, as always, to take responsibility for
everything done by the men of the navy while I had the incompa-
rable honor of being their commander in chief. I also take
responsibility for the men of the security and police forces." He
extended that responsibility "to the errors that may have been
committed" by his subordinates.

"I and I alone have the right to sit in the defendant's seat," he
boasted, his gaze fixed on the six judges.

Nonetheless, he did not acknowledge any of the acts that took
place on his orders. "I feel responsible, but I do not feel guilty,"
he said, before reaching the following Olympian conclusion:
"My judges may control the daily news, but I am in command of
history, and that is where the final verdict will be heard."

Responsibility without guilt, the isolated mistakes of subordinates, which are assumed in the serene consciousness of a historical mandate. The same rhetorical smokescreen as always. Scilingo is irritated at the memory of it. What kept him from sleeping, as much or more than the flights, was the persistent hypocrisy of the men who ordered him to carry them out.

Chapter Eleven
All or None

THE ARMED forces had grudgingly accepted the prosecution of their former leaders without ever acknowledging their guilt. But the officers on active duty, the direct executors of the atrocious and aberrant acts ordered by their superiors, threatened an uprising each time the arm of the law pointed toward them. With the same logic as Scilingo, they would see themselves only as cogs in a hierarchical, institutional machine, whose responsibility would have to be collective and could not be measured by the yardstick of the civil penal code, which sets forth punishments for criminal acts committed by individuals of their own free will.

The warrant for the arrest of Captains Gustavo Adolfo Alsina and Enrique Mones Ruiz precipitated the first military crisis in the army, in June 1984. The arrest of Astiz did the same in the navy, six months later.

Alsina was put on trial for the torture and death of Dr. José

René Moukarzel, who was placed in stocks in a prison courtyard in freezing weather as a punishment for having received a packet of salt from another prisoner. For twelve hours he was beaten and buckets of water were thrown on his naked body. When he was taken to the infirmary, Alsina prevented anyone from attending to him. When a soldier informed him of the death of the tortured man, Alsina answered, "Congratulations, you've just killed a subversive." A prison official threw the doctor's eyeglasses into his former cell and announced to his cellmates: "That's all that's left of the Turk."

Mones Ruiz had to answer for the murder of the prisoner Raúl Augusto Bauducco, a murder that is representative of the arbitrary way in which human life was taken. During a tour of inspection, Bauducco was beaten with rubber batons and forced to remain with his arms against the wall. After two hours he could no longer maintain the position.

"Raise them or I'll kill you," Corporal Miguel Angel Pérez screamed at him.

"I can't, sir," Bauducco answered. Pérez requested permission. Mones Ruiz gave it to him. The noncommissioned officer shot the prisoner in the head point-blank. "Bauducco tried to take the gun away," Mones Ruiz later reported.

A group of officers threatened a large-scale rebellion as a way of asking a federal judge to stop bothering their comrades. His honor was not insensitive to their pleas and transferred the proceedings to a military court, which gave instructions for Mones Ruiz and Alsina to be set free.

The officers at ESMA took the names of animals as aliases. Chamorro was "the Dolphin," Acosta "the Tiger," Pernías "the Rat," Astiz "the Raven," and Scilingo doesn't remember. The second crisis was provoked when charges were brought against the Raven by another federal judge during the torrid December of 1984 and this crisis lasted throughout the subsequent summer. The Council of Admirals convened and demanded that

Astiz not be subjected to a lineup or to any confrontation with witnesses and that he be allowed to present himself in uniform—a point of honor for the navy—though the complaint stated that when he abducted Swedish teenager Dagmar Ingrid Hagelin he was wearing civilian clothing. This trial, too, was transferred to a military court, which absolved Astiz. The ruling was appealed to the Federal Chamber of Appeals, which held that although Astiz's participation in the kidnapping had been proven, the action against him was invalid because of the amount of time that had elapsed. This type of compromise was typical of Alfonsín's government: guilty but allowed to go free.

Three of the Mothers of the Plaza de Mayo, with their white handkerchiefs on their heads, waited for the judges to leave the courtroom, then shouted "Murderer!" and "Monster!" as Astiz went past. One of them had witnessed the abduction of the nuns and the ten family members of *desaparecidos* Astiz had betrayed with his kisses. From the back of the courtroom, one of Astiz's comrades in arms ordered, "Why don't they arrest that Marxist whore?"

The bailiff obeyed him.

When the time limit set by the Full Stop law was up, formal accusations had been processed against four hundred officers from the three armed services and from law enforcement agencies across the country. That number was fifteen times higher than the military had hoped and three or four times greater than its most pessimistic projections. The ESMA survivors identified one hundred and ten men stationed there who were responsible for four hundred cases, less than a tenth of all cases under investigation. The state prosecutor asked that only thirty-three of those officers be brought to trial, and the Federal Chamber agreed to bring only nineteen of them to trial, including six retired admirals and six officers on active duty. Among the latter were Astiz, Pernías, and the noncommissioned officer Antonio Azic, who had used the electric cattle prod on a twenty-day-old baby, the son of a prisoner.

The comrades of Mones Ruiz, Alsina, Pernías, Rolón, Scilingo, and Astiz went so far as to contemplate forming commando groups in order to resist the summonses and rescue Massera and Videla from prison. Pernías led an attempted uprising, which was checked by a persuasive comrade who spent an entire sleepless night convincing him that the navy as an institution would defend its men.

During a meeting of his cabinet, President Alfonsín proposed an escalation of measures to put down any uprising:

1. Discharge of any unit leader who gives asylum to an insurrectionist and does not guarantee handing him over to the courts.
2. Siege of any rebel unit with troops from the same branch of the armed forces and eventual recourse to troops from the other two branches if that is unavoidable.
3. Cutting off of food supplies, water, electricity, and gas.
4. National and international media campaign.
5. Public mobilization against the insurrectionists.
6. Use of weapons to subjugate them.

The navy's chief of staff presented a counterproposal: the navy would negotiate with the government as to an acceptable number of men to be placed on trial. It would have to be far fewer than was currently planned, and it was imperative to remove the symbolic Astiz from the list. The government refused. At 2:30 A.M. on Wednesday, February 25, 1984, the chief of staff sent a radiogram countersigned by the entire admiralty to units across the country. He described the situation as extremely serious because indictments were being bought against "certain of its men for a participation that extends to the entire navy." Nevertheless, the six retired admirals duly arrived at the courthouse under arrest, in a navy van and under the supervision of the general director of personnel. As in the dirty war, the navy continued to act vertically, in fulfillment of orders from the higher ranks. The following day, when he brought in the remaining men who were under arrest, the navy's chief of intelligence warned one of the judges: "You are applying the penal code, but some of these men have seen me do worse things than those you are judging them for."

It was the same message Scilingo would repeat later: since many men did it, though there isn't evidence against all of them, none should be punished.

Chapter Twelve
Modus Operandi

IN THE unsworn statement he made to the Federal Chamber, Commander Jorge Eduardo Acosta, the former chief of intelligence of the ESMA task force, said that the school had been the unit especially designated to combat the Montoneros. The prosecutor asked him how many of them had been held at ESMA.

"I don't really have the precise number, but I would say, sir, that . . ." Acosta began to answer. Then he hesitated and asked for a significant clarification: "Including the dead ones?"

After thinking it over a long time, he answered that between 1976 and 1979, three hundred to five hundred prisoners had been rotated through ESMA. He classified them into two groups. If it was decided that they had no link to the guerrilla group, they were set free. After 1977, the decision was made not to kill the militants but to try to transform them into naval intelligence agents who would help bring the confrontation quickly to an end, he said. (Admirals Massera, Lambruschini, and

Mendía had taken offense at the very suggestion that prisoners might have taken part in intelligence tasks.)

"There was no one in between the two groups, who did have something to do with the Montoneros but refused to collaborate with you?" the court asked Acostá.

"There may have been. In that case, I believe they were . . . I know of some who were handed over to the Executive Power or, but I . . . What finally happened to them I don't know," Acosta floundered.

"Do you recall any individual case, of a person who may have been turned over to the Executive Power?" the prosecutor pressed him.

"Yes . . . it's Mrs. . . . a very young woman . . . whose husband . . . I can't tell you the surname, but maybe if I check I can give you the exact name. I think that her father was a noncommissioned army officer and he provided information that his daughter was in the terrorist organization so then she was picked up. She said, 'No, I'm not participating, I don't believe in any of that,' and went to the Executive Power."

Placement at the disposition of the Executive Power is an exceptional measure authorized by the Argentine Constitution in cases of external war or internal disruption and implies the suspension of individual rights and guarantees. During the military dictatorship, being placed in that situation was the equivalent of having one's life saved, because that way there was at least a record of the arrest. According to ESMA's chief of intelligence himself, this occurred once, out of five hundred cases. As for the rest, "Other organizations I don't know anything about came to get them."

The court wished to know how the fate of each prisoner was determined. Acosta described a mock trial in which life and death were at stake: "Something very similar to this, with all due respect, was convened. The commander and his staff were there. The prosecutor was the operations officer and the defense attorney was the intelligence man. They took opposite positions. The operations man told what the prisoner said when arrested. The intelligence man argued that the prisoner said it because he was faking. And it went like that until the determination was reached," Acosta answered.

With the arrest of Acosta, Astiz, Pernías, and the other navy men, a countdown began that would culminate two months later. The navy conducted itself with a degree of institutional unity, that explains the difficulty even men like Scilingo, who were disillusioned by their superior officers, would have detaching themselves from the its discipline and its myths.

The army, on the other hand, fell apart.

"My jacket was stained in the dirty war, too," said a general from the Superior School of War.

"With tomato sauce," whispered a captain, the son of one of the generals who had been charged.

Seventy army officers on active duty demonstrated in the military quarter of Buenos Aires in solidarity with Mones Ruiz — who had once again been summoned by the courts — beneath a summer cloudburst. Some of them wore their uniforms and complained about the military leadership.

A week later, no less a personage than the aide to the chief of staff of the army, a lieutenant colonel on active duty, was arrested for aggravated homicide and accused of having shot three prisoners on the pretext that they were trying to escape. The very perversion of the system that was applied, the exemplary pretensions of barbarity itself, was what finally allowed light to be shed on this event.

The only survivor of the incident told the courts about the operation. Four prisoners were taken by the army officer from a prison in the province of Córdoba. The prison's female employees demanded that a receipt be signed before handing them over. After they had gone down a stretch of road, the lieutenant colonel had the prisoners taken out of the truck in which they were being transported. The prisoner heard him say, "Prepare your weapons." Then the officer asked his men if they were ready. When he received an affirmative response, he ordered them to open fire. The prisoner heard shots and guttural sounds from someone who couldn't scream because he was gagged.

"This work is for shit," said one of the men who were doing the shooting.

"Get used to it—that's how war is," his commanding officer answered.

An officer removed the blindfold and gag from the remaining prisoner and led him to the fallen body of one of his comrades, which had a bullet hole in the right eyebrow. The bodies of the other two prisoners were lying a few steps away.

"Do you know why we killed them?" the officer asked. "Because you guys killed a corporal."

"I don't agree with killing anybody."

"It's too late for that. Now, when you go back to the jail, you'll tell the others everything you saw. Let them know that if they keep killing soldiers the same thing is going to happen to all of them. And you are number one on the list. Today you just barely got away with your life."

One of the men who was shot was the prisoner's brother.

The agitated young officers who did not accept being put on trial turned against the chief of staff of the army, who was not even capable of defending his own aide. Alsina and Mones Ruiz went to the media with a declaration stating, "The current top ranks of the military were part of the armed forces during the war against subversion and held posts of significant power. The due process which they did not demand from the successive military juntas they now seek to impose on subalterns who limited themselves to a strict compliance with orders." The third man accompanying them on that risky mission was Lieutenant Colonel Ernesto Guillermo Barreiro, a.k.a. "Nabo" (Fool), who had as obvious an interest as they did in the matter: charges had been filed against him for his performance as the head torturer at La Perla, the concentration camp in Córdoba.

Another dangerous task was assigned to an officer who, accompanied by a group of young men, showed up wearing fatigues and a helmet in the Plaza de Mayo at the time of the Mothers' weekly rounds. "Freedom for the heroes of the war against subversion. Enough leftist trials. Freedom to our liberators," said their placards. Hebe Bonafini chased after them with a megaphone, shouting "Stool pigeons!" and "Cuckolds!" The Circle of Military Men stood by the "young men who only acted out of the fullness of their patriotic fervor" in pursuing their adversaries.

All three of the armed forces were wrenched by heated arguments about the responsibility of the superiors who gave the orders and the subordinates who executed them. A week before public hearings began in the trial of Pernías, Astiz, and the other men from the navy who had been charged, the crisis in the army exploded. On Wednesday, April 15, 1987, Lieutenant Colonel Barreiro did not arrive at his appointment with the judges and took refuge in an infantry regiment, whose commanding officer refused to arrest him. The other units in the garrison did not carry out the order to take him prisoner. A paratrooper captain explained the position of the rebels to the press: "We are being judged by people who don't even understand us. We military men have our modus operandi, too."

The largest military garrison in Buenos Aires was taken over by Lieutenant Colonel Aldo Rico. The rebellion of the soldiers with painted faces, the *carapintadas*, began in Easter Week 1987. In front of the legislative assembly and a few yards away from a crowd of hundreds of thousands of people that had gathered in the street outside. President Alfonsín proclaimed, "The democracy of the Argentine people is not open to negotiation."

But Rico warned that there would be no officers in the entire army who were prepared to arrest him.

"I'm going to get you out of there with cannon fire," threat-ened the general who was in charge of putting down the uprising.

"As soon as you do that, I'll fire a mortar into the crowd (which had gathered outside the garrison), and it will be up to you to explain that it wasn't your cannon that was badly aimed," Rico answered him. The general, who had also partici-pated in the dirty war, did not insist upon the issue and his troops never achieved their objective.

That afternoon, approximately two thousand unarmed people were on the point of entering the rebel garrison, to put pressure on the commandos. When he realized that he was los-ing control of the situation, Alfonsín rushed to the site. On his return to the Plaza de Mayo after a dialogue with the rebel leader, he received an ovation from the crowd when he announced that "the mutinying men have changed their stance." But there was bewilderment and sharp whistles of disapproval when he added that among them were heroes of the Malvinas war, who had adopted a mistaken position without any inten-tion of causing a coup d'etat—exactly the opposite of what he had said to Congress. He concluded by asking the civilians who had entered the military garrison to withdraw, as the grand finale to an impressive political sleight of hand.

The upshot of all this was the law of Due Obedience, more a judicial ruling than a law, as was noted by the only judge on the Argentine Supreme Court who had the courage to declare it unconstitutional. The text of the law stated that all military men of a given rank would be exculpated for having obeyed the orders of their superiors. With that law, Alfonsín was able to ful-fill his objective of excusing the aberrant and atrocious acts that had been committed against helpless prisoners. Congress approved the law under pressure from the military, and during the last week of June 1987, most of the military men who were being held on criminal charges recovered their freedom, among them Astiz and Pernías.

With his pardons of 1990 and 1991, Menem cut the knot that Alfonsín had begun to untie. But not even then did they succeed in turning over the most tragic page of modern Argentine history. Various human rights organizations demanded the discharge of all those pardoned. They were beyond the reach of the law, but there was no reason why they should be rewarded. At the end of every year, the battle began anew with the nominations for promotions from each branch of the armed forces.

During the proceedings against him, Astiz remained at the same rank. But in a demonstration of solidarity, the junior officers who had risen above him treated him as a superior, out of sympathy for what they called the destruction of his career and his life. "I was repudiated socially in various circles. I couldn't even visit my parents," Astiz complained to the military court during a hearing. In the following years, the gossip magazines would photograph him several times dancing in Buenos Aires discothèques. He went so far as to hit journalists and photographers, expose their film, and break their cameras.

In a dramatic news release sent to its subscribers throughout the world on Christmas Eve 1987, the France Press news agency alleged that "Astiz represents a veritable time bomb sitting on the desk of the head of state. The entire Argentine navy, from the lowest cabinboy to the officers of the high command, was mobilized behind Astiz to see to it that President Raúl Alfonsín authorized his promotion, under the threat of unleashing a new rebellion should he reject it." Alfonsín acceded to their demands, but simultaneously instructed the minister of defense to begin procedures to force Astiz into retirement.

According to Alfonsín's instructions, the promotion of an officer absolved by the courts could not be refused. But since Astiz, "for reasons that may or may not have been voluntary," had taken on special significance for the society, which condemns the methods of the terrorist state, his presence on active duty could pose a threat to the social fabric and have negative repercussions on the military institutions. For that reason, "he must not remain on active duty."

Behind this intricate piece of reasoning was concealed the basic fact that Astiz's absolution by the courts was not related to his innocence but only to a law that came after the trial and was passed specifically to rescue him from jail. The claim that Astiz's sad notoriety had nothing to do with his own will is as unfair to him as it is to the victims who were deprived of the conclusion of the judicial process in which almost complete proof was presented of his guilt in the atrocious crime of abducting two nuns and ten family members of disappeared persons.

He was not removed from active duty because he was guilty, but because he was too well known. Being less notorious, the other three hundred kidnappers, torturers, and murderers who benefited from the law of Due Obedience had not only remained free of prosecution under the penal code, but could continue their military careers.

The navy did not comply with the order to retire Astiz. Pernías appeared on the list of promotions that Alfonsín signed without quibbling. But not only Pernías. A journalist who would later become the director of Menem's intelligence service pointed out the contradiction between the order of retirement for Astiz and the simultaneous promotion to vice admiral of Adolfo Mario Arduino, who had been Astiz's superior at ESMA and was also accused of human rights violations.

Arduino was the superior officer who, one day in 1977, ordered Scilingo to prepare for his first flight.

Part III
Alienation

Chapter Thirteen
Whiskey and Pills

HE DRANK two glasses of whiskey, brim-full, when he came back from the first flight. He drank each down in one long gulp and slept until the next day. This medicine brought him more consolation than the naval chaplain's words. But it didn't numb him enough. Later he gave up alcohol for psychopharmacological drugs. Whether with whiskey or sleeping pills, the hardest thing was getting through the night. As soon as he fell asleep, he relived the flight. While he was throwing the naked bodies out the hatch, he missed his step and fell. That day in 1977 a member of the crew had managed to hold him back. But as soon as he fell asleep, he was devoured by empty space. Before he reached the ocean's waters, he would wake up.

Nevertheless, it took many years before Scilingo began to question the order that sent him on that flight. His initial criticisms were of other matters that seemed more serious to him at the time.

Everything that was seized during the house searches was stored in a warehouse at the school. Careful records were kept. According to regulations, an object could be taken out only for a task force's operational requirements or in order to help the widow of a dead colleague. One day Scilingo went to the store-room to get a drill he needed for the auto shop and discovered it wasn't there.

"But there used to be two or three of them," he complained, to no avail.

He began to observe that the control of those goods had become much laxer. He brought the subject up with his superiors, and they told him it was not his concern. He was also critical of the excessive amounts of money being spent on automotive services. Vehicles were not being taken care of, and luxury features were requested that were unheard-of for cars used in covert operations. He even received complaints because the auto shop delivered a car that was missing a strip of metal trim on one side and another with a flaw in its upholstery. Intelligence vehicles had top priority, though they were not always used for intelligence tasks. All requests and complaints were conveyed to him by the officer in charge of the parking lot, Lieutenant Vaca, his companion during the first flight, with whom Scilingo was developing a reciprocal antipathy.

According to Scilingo, the prisoners were stripped naked before they were thrown out of the plane, but the first corpses that appeared in Uruguay were clothed. "That was really fucked up, the worst atrocity. The guy who did that flight went crazy. He couldn't take it and asked to be discharged," Scilingo says, by way of an explanation. He doesn't want to elaborate.

"Before I talk about that I have to check on something."

"*What?*"

"A name."

"*When you went into the torture chamber and saw Lieutenant Vaca's woman lawyer . . .*"

"I'm not going to tell you anything more until I've checked on that name."

"Did they throw her out clothed? And not only clothed, did they throw them out while they were conscious?"

"Once I'm sure of that name we'll talk about this again."

Scilingo was starting to become a troublesome figure. He was transferred from the Navy School of Mechanics in 1978, to the frigate *Liberty*, where he was in charge of propulsion and electricity. Then he was put in charge of engines on the destroyer *Storni*, was made second in command of the *Sobral*, a dispatch boat, and was subsequently put in command of a torpedo launcher in Tierra del Fuego, at the utmost end of the earth. He rose to the rank of lieutenant commander without any problem. He carried out his duties like anyone else, without calling attention to himself, and he was never reprimanded. But inside him, nothing would ever be the same as before the flight.

At the Puerto Belgrano naval base, he crossed paths with the former chief of intelligence of ESMA again. Commander Jorge Acosta drove through the officers' district in a Mercedes Benz, and his house was being renovated by a team of decorators. What had become of Admiral Mayorga's gold watch?

From Tierra del Fuego, Scilingo was transferred to a desk job as an aide to the director of the Military House of the Presidency. He arrived at the Pink House two days before Videla retired, and remained there under the military dictators Viola, Galtieri, and Bignone and for the first five months of President Alfonsín's administration. Those were the years when the economic euphoria known euphemistically as the "easy money" came to an end, the years of the Malvinas war, the collapse of the dictatorship, and the revelations about unidentified corpses in the press—which was suddenly observing things as if it had just arrived in a foreign country—the years of the "Final Document of the Military Junta . . . ," the military's autoamnesty and its repeal, the investigations of the Commission on the Disappeared, the trial of the former military leaders, and the first charges against Astiz. The disappeared and those who had made them disappear occupied center stage in the country's political arena. Scilingo's ghosts had now become corporeal.

But he also had other worries, which he brought up with his boss. His experience as an electrician had been acquired on technological systems that were now outmoded, and his operative background was also too out of date to allow him to play a role within a modern unit. The fact that his technical and operative skills were not current could jeopardize his future. He wanted to be transferred to a post that would train him in the new systems or to a unit in the Antarctic. Five months later, with high hopes, he received an order transferring him to the Argentine navy's only aircraft carrier.

Born in Bahía Blanca, home of the country's largest naval base, Scilingo was one of three children. His father was a small-time builder, and his mother was a schoolteacher. For him, a career in the navy had been the obvious ambition from the start. Now his lengthy posting behind a desk at the Military House of the Presidency was not going to ruin that career, which still seemed to him to be the best and only one possible.

Scilingo was supposed to take the entrance examination for the Navy School of War in order to take the staff course, and he did not feel up to it. Three weeks before the exam, he notified the chief of the naval arsenal that his schedule and duties at the Military House of the Presidency had not allowed him to prepare for it, and he requested a year's deferment in order "to have the same chance as the rest of the officers taking the exam."

The arsenal chief rejected the request. There was very little time to look into the case before the exam, and the request was unprecedented. Moreover, passage through the School of War had ceased to be a requirement for occupying command posts or being promoted. Scilingo was urged to redouble his preparations in the two weeks remaining before the exam. A copy of his request and of the response to it were sent to the School of War.

Scilingo took the exam. Later he met with the school's staff. They asked him why he had requested a deferment since he was well prepared (which was how he learned he had done well on the exam). He decided to speak frankly.

"The real story is this: when I'm under stress I get blocked because of an incident that happened when I was at ESMA during the war against subversion," he said.

He told them about his nightmare. After an interminable silence, a superior officer advised him, "You should see someone about that."

"I don't know if I need to see anyone," he answered, surprised.

"We suggest you see someone," the officer repeated.

On his return to Puerto Belgrano, he found his commanding officer in a bad mood. "I think you talked too much at the School of War."

"Why do you say that?"

"You brought something up that's going to cause you some problems," his boss answered, handing him an order to undergo psychiatric evaluation.

At the Naval Hospital he was given a series of tests. The result: he was not ill nor was he suffering from psychiatric problems that would render him unfit for duty. Nevertheless, in a confidential memo barely eighty words long, he was told he had not qualified for entrance to the Navy School of War. With a profusion of capital letters typical of naval prose, the memo said that he was "permanently not recommended for directive functions," and was "recommended to remain on active duty." This meant that his career would end with no further promotions because he had been "definitively excluded from the front ranks of lieutenant commanders who will be considered by the Qualifications Board." Right about then, the public hearings in the trial of the former military leaders had concluded, and the judges were evaluating the evidence and drafting their ruling.

In the navy, the decisions of superiors are not questioned. Scilingo could ask only that the decision be reconsidered. He explained that in his various posts he had received high ratings. He wrote that no one had ever objected to his ethical or professional qualities, his personality, his leadership capacity, his performance in general, and his psychological and physical aptitude for duty. He had always been recommended for command functions, his record was clean, and he had never even received a verbal reprimand. He also tried to put his dialogue with the staff of the Navy School of War in perspective: his nerves had been jangled by fatigue, overwork in his position as aide to the director of the Military House of the Presidency, the loss of his annual vacation, and the situation the country and the navy were in following the rise to power of elected officials who were putting the former military leaders on trial.

He said that during that interview he had referred to an "atypical" and "strictly personal" problem. It had been overcome and had never affected his professional conduct. The file he submitted included the test results declaring him psychiatrically exonerated and the favorable reviews of his direct superiors "with respect to my aptitude for command or directive functions."

But not even in this bureaucratic memo, written to beg that his career not be cut short, was he able to omit the facts that had frightened his superiors. "This situation originated in an event that occurred during a flight made in a Skyvan plane belonging to the Argentine coast guard in the year 1977, in which, while carrying out activities related to the war against subversion and while the plane's hatch was open, I lost my balance and was about to fall out into empty space, an event that was prevented by the rapid intervention of a member of the crew," he wrote.

He had passed through a bad time, but now he was back on his feet and he wouldn't let his tongue wag again in front of anyone, friend or stranger, was the implicit message. Three weeks later he had his response, which was even shorter than the initial notification. Now he was "temporarily not recommended for directive functions." In other words, he would not be promoted this year, but he could be considered for promotion the following year. No doubt remained as to what the problem was that had made him seem untrustworthy in the eyes of his superiors.

A few days later, the Federal Chamber condemned Videla and Massera to life imprisonment without possibility of parole and discharged them from the armed forces, as the agents of multiple homicides aggravated by the defenselessness of the victims, illegal detentions exacerbated by threats and violence, torture, and torture followed by death and robbery.

The ruling described the "criminal plan" adopted by the former military leaders which consisted of "apprehending suspects, keeping them secretly in captivity under inhuman conditions, subjecting them to torture in the name of obtaining information, and finally turning them over to the courts or the National Executive Power, or else eliminating them physically."

In their defense, the military leaders admitted, in the same terms as in the "Final Document," the possibility that excesses may have been committed, which were justified by the existence of an unconventional war. The Federal Chamber's response to this was that "the seriousness of the guerrilla problem and the difficulty of combatting it cannot be admissible reasons for committing acts that demonstrated absolute contempt for human dignity." According to the judges, "killing an enemy on the battlefield and in the heat of battle bears no resemblance whatsoever to applying cruel torture to helpless people within the calm security of four walls." The court maintained that not even blind obedience could excuse those who obeyed the orders to commit atrocities, whatever their rank. "Respect for the person of the captured enemy constitutes an essential rule, which cannot be absent from the mind of any member of the military and which has been consecrated by international norms and domestic law."

The court was punishing the kidnappings, the tortures and the secret killings. Meanwhile, the navy was reprehending those who mentioned those acts, even among colleagues. Massera was supposed to spend the rest of his life in jail; meanwhile, Scilingo could go on with his career because, once more, he had recovered his balance just before falling.

But Scilingo had another surprise in store for his superiors: he voluntarily requested retirement. He couldn't stand the silence any longer.

Chapter Fourteen
A Subject of No Importance

HIS SUPERIOR on the aircraft carrier was Captain Jorge Osvaldo Ferrer, who listened to him without expression or comment. After Scilingo's request for reconsideration was accepted, Ferrer was the first to learn that Scilingo was thinking of asking for retirement. Ferrer said only that he would try to facilitate the process.

When Videla demanded that his actions during the dirty war be vindicated, Scilingo wrote his first letter. By then, Ferrer was an admiral and the chief of staff of the navy. He did not even acknowledge receipt of the two letters Scilingo sent him.

Ferrer and the assistant chief were out of the country when Scilingo sent his first letter. The director of personnel at that time, Fausto López, was third in command. The day the letter was received, a close friend of Scilingo's was about to assume a command post in Puerto Belgrano. He was forced to postpone the celebration of his new command and go to Buenos Aires to find out what Scilingo was trying to accomplish with his letters. The friend had trouble carrying out the mission.

"I've been ordered to ask you if you want money," he confessed in embarrassment.

"Don't get involved in this," Scilingo answered.

Fausto López then summoned Scilingo to a meeting and warned him that it was inappropriate for him to mention such matters.

"What are you trying to achieve?" López asked.

"The only thing I want is an answer."

"What you are doing is dangerous. Think of your family. You could lose your naval benefits."

"To me, it was unacceptable for the navy to think I had made a mistake or had some problem with the flights, that I couldn't acknowledge to my superiors that at a given moment the subject was disturbing to me. If I hadn't told the truth to my superiors—not my enemies, my superiors, staff officers—it's likely I would still be on active duty and my name would be sent to the Confirmation Committee," Scilingo reflected. As soon as possible, he dropped the naval benefits and took out private medical insurance.

When he learned that he could not hope for answers from his former superiors and comrades, he began to seek them outside the navy, but without much more success. Just as he had told Ferrer and Menem he would, he went to the prosecutors' office of the Federal Chamber. "I don't know what I was looking for. Someone who would pay attention to the matter. I'm not saying I need to make a public confession or justify myself—that's not it at all. I want to get out from inside me something I did, which my superiors have made me think was something bad."

He was heard by Luis Moreno Ocampo, who had been the prosecutor of Videla, Massera, Pernías, and Astiz and had then sided in favor of the constitutionality of the pardons. "I went to talk to him because I needed to understand why this was not being brought to light once and for all. Moreno Ocampo was stretched out in a big leather chair with his feet on a little table. He was very attentive, but it didn't go any further than that. Something's happening here that might be difficult for a lot of people to understand, but the reality is that this subject, I don't know if it's taboo, but everyone wants to forget about it." He told his story and showed the documentation. He says that Moreno Ocampo listened to him and suggested he go to a publisher. "I got the impression he didn't care."

The former prosecutor remembers the conversation differently. "He came with his wife. First he said he had only taken a few prisoners out to finger their comrades in the street. Then later he said he had also taken part in kidnapping. And when it was his turn to participate in a flight, he discovered that the man he had kidnapped was on board the airplane. Despite the injection, the prisoner woke up to semiconsciousness, resisted being thrown out, and almost dragged him down with him into empty space. After the Due Obedience law and the pardon there was no possibility of opening up a judicial investigation. He asked me to put him in touch with *Somos* magazine, but I didn't want to get involved. His motives were very mixed: the memory kept him from sleeping, the navy was conducting a preliminary hearing on something he had done, and he also wanted money for telling his story."

Scilingo went to *Somos* magazine. He knew its editor in chief, to whom he had given some documents obtained at the Pink House which were used in a series of articles on the Malvinas war. He says the editor in chief answered that the flights were "a subject we don't deal with." But not because it was of no importance to them: the navy was informed of his visit to the magazine. "It seems they weren't interested," Scilingo was mocked.

The former editor of the magazine denies this. He says Scilingo offered to tell his story for ten thousand dollars, which he needed in order to set up his cable television system; when they asked for some time to think it over, he disappeared saying he would go to *Noticias* magazine.

And that is what Scilingo says he did: "I was met by a young lady who directed me to another young lady who said she was the assistant editor or something like that, and she told me I might want to write a letter to the editor." In any case, Scilingo's principal concern, when his confessions were recorded as the basis for this book, was to make it known that he was not speaking out of self-interest: "I haven't sold out." He requested only legal support in case of any litigation with the navy.

He had tried the navy, the federal government, the courts, and the press. There remained only the Congress. When Pernías and Rolón were summoned by the Senate, Scilingo made copies of all his letters and sent them to each one of the members of the Confirmation Committee. This had no effect either.

"The matter of the disappeared was very important to me. It may be that the navy, the majority of journalists and the majority of the public consider it a subject of no importance," he muses.

With two partners ("they're Jews," he notes) he now exports fermented cider and suede bikinis to Brazil. Scilingo tries to smile, "Maybe I'm mistaken, and you are, too, to waste your time on me."

Part IV
Catharsis

Chapter Fifteen
A Surface Smoothed Down by Death

IN 1981, the Argentine writer Julio Cortázar published the plot of a short story in the *Revista de Occidente* in Madrid:

> A group of Argentines decides to found a city on a promising stretch of level ground, without realizing that most of the land on which they are starting to build their houses is a cemetery of which no visible trace remains. Only the leaders know this, and they keep quiet about it because the place fits in with their plans, because it is a surface smoothed down by death and silence. So buildings and streets go up and life is organized and prospers; very quickly the city reaches considerable heights and proportions, and its lights, which can be seen from very far away, are the proud symbol of those who erected the new metropolis. It is then that the symptoms of a strange unease begin, the fears and suspicions of those who feel that strange forces are pursuing them and in some way denouncing them and trying to drive them away. The most sensitive among them finally understand that they are living on top of death, and that the dead know how to come back, in their own way,

and to enter the houses, the dreams, the happiness of the city's inhabitants. What seemed to be the realization of one of the ideals of our times—I mean a triumph of technology, of modern life enveloped in the cotton wadding of televisions, refrigerators, movie theaters and an abundance of money and patriotic self-satisfaction—slowly awakes to the worst of nightmares, to the cold and viscous presence of invisible rebukes, of a malediction that is not expressed in words but that taints with its unspeakable horror everything these men built atop a necropolis.

Cortázar said he did not write the story because he found out it had already been written in the book of history. But in a fantastically Cortazarian denouement, history rewrote it fifteen years later.

Scilingo was not mistaken, nor was talking to him a waste of time. The publication of his words had an electrical effect that ran through Argentine society's every cell. Argentina awoke to the worst of nightmares. Scilingo said nothing that was not already known, but the words of an executioner admitting to his crimes in the first person had an extraordinary impact, as if the exhibition of Scilingo's tormented soul were necessary to put an end to the two different versions of Argentine history in circulation, in circulation, so that the narrative of the victims would cease to be that of pariahs and madmen and become the common sense of society.

The Spanish edition of *The Flight* was published in Buenos Aires on March 2, 1995. The country's leading television talk show broadcast excerpts from my recorded dialogues with Scilingo, which were broadcast again the next morning by several radio stations. Their switchboards were jammed by an unprecedented number of calls from the public.

That day, the navy was to pay homage to its patron, an Irish admiral who fought in the nineteenth-century wars of independence. But the chief of staff deserted the traditional ceremony. The admirals remained alone, standing in formation in the street beneath the summer sun, surrounding two army guests who had been invited to the celebration which could not begin without the chief of staff. Two very high ranking generals, both of them more than six feet, five inches tall, stood out in their green uniforms in the ocean of blue jackets worn by the bewildered men of the navy. A hundred or so journalists pounced on the highest ranking admiral present:

"What will the navy's response be?" they asked him.

He could defend himself only with a phrase that tried to be severe but sounded ridiculous: "No, no microphone soup."

Then he confessed that he didn't know what to say, slammed the door of his car, and left. Microphone soup is a very nourishing dish for young, growing democracies.

Admiral Molina Pico, the chief of staff, had left for the same airport from which Scilingo went on his first flight, urgently summoned by President Menem during a stopover on the campaign trail so that Molina Pico could inform him of what was going on. At the airport, the president maintained that Scilingo was "a scoundrel" whose statements were not trustworthy because he was facing "various charges for falsification, fraud, and car theft." He went on to attribute the publication of the book to "interests linked to the electoral campaign." Molina Pico sent a secret radiogram to his subordinates, in which he recommended that they remain silent in order to keep the matter from resonating any further.

From London, the Holocaust investigator Zygmunt Bauman commented, "What did they expect, that after throwing thirty people alive into the sea he would dedicate himself to cultivating his garden?"

The president and the chief of staff sought to bring down to the level of their own banality a transcendent episode whose richness escaped them. Nevertheless, Scilingo and the disappeared, the role of the military and of the Church, truth and justice, quickly occupied the center of the political debate in Argentina, displacing the issues of the electoral campaign.

The chain reaction started by Scilingo spread to the Catholic Church. In response to his assertion that the method of the flight had been approved by Church authorities and that the chaplains comforted the officers after their missions, various bishops requested forgiveness for the cowardice or complicity of some among them, and the Conference of Bishops maintained that any member of the Church who had supported the actions "would have acted on his personal responsibility, erring or sinning seriously."

The discussion even extended to the activities during the dictatorship of Pío Laghi, the former apostolic nuncio, who would later become the first ambassador of the Vatican to the United States and is now mentioned as a prospective pope. Moved by Scilingo's confession and its extraordinary social repercussions, the wives of two disappeared men revealed that the pope's representative had knowledge of the lists of the disappeared and that a high ranking naval officer had once consulted Laghi on the question of what to do with four dozen *desaparecidos* whom the officer didn't want to kill but couldn't make up his mind to free either.

One of the women was the wife and business partner of the journalist Julián Delgado. Delgado was the editor of several business publications and a supporter of the military government's economic policies, and he fell in the crossfire between opposing factions of the dictatorship for reasons that were not political but financial. His wife said that previously she had taken action only for her husband's sake, but after Scilingo's confession "all the disappeared are important to me. Now I talk about our disappeared. Because there is a problem in this society. It seems as if the disappeared are *them*, not *us*. They are ours, they are us." She explained that Pío Laghi "would have done what was necessary for my husband, he would have taken him out in one of those cars with diplomatic plates, but other people did not have the same luck. And a man who knows that there are forty living people, and who has brought out some people who have been liberated as a result of many steps he has taken on their behalf, also knows that there are other people, too, many more of them, who haven't gotten out. And since the time of justice has passed, this is the time of truth. I call it my second chance, and it is also many people's second chance, and I don't want to waste it. Before I acted, but I didn't see these things as clearly. I know they are useful, for other people and for the society as a whole, and that's why I can't keep quiet about them."

While on one Buenos Aires radio station Cardinal Laghi explained from Rome that "we didn't know what was happening," a bishop on another station told the story of how, through Laghi's intervention, someone who was "being pursued by the whole army" was able to leave the country. No one tried to explain the nonsensical logic of someone who was working for human rights, saving lives, taking people who were being hunted to the airport, and at the same time didn't know what was going on. From a distance and after many years had gone by, Laghi didn't see how much Argentine society had changed, and he repeated the old official discourse, which was no longer tenable.

Several witnesses had said that the former nuncio periodically played tennis with Massera, and a bishop explained that by citing Laghi's fanatical devotion to the game. To top it all off, the discharged and pardoned former admiral broke his ten-year silence to defend the good name of his tennis partner in the face of so many "slanderous news reports" and attested to Laghi's concern over the fate of "the so-called disappeared."

The flash of illumination finally came from the Church itself, when Bishop Miguel Esteban Hesayne (the same man who had confronted the military and denounced torture as anti-Christian) said in a shattering Easter message that, "lamentably, repentance still has not touched all those it should touch, including the Conference of Bishops itself," which, he claimed, "has sat down to eat with those we called torturers. We have received them in the heart of the Conference of Bishops so that they could excuse themselves, or rather so that they could try to deceive us by claiming that these were merely excesses. Furthermore, we did not want to receive the mothers of the disappeared, who for a whole day, under the rain, stood at the doors of the Plenary Assembly of the Bishopric. And as we were saying then with another bishop, what must Jesus Christ be saying at this moment, when we do not listen to the pleas of mothers?" Sent out early on Good Friday, Hesayne's letter put an end to the polemic. Profoundly divided, the Bishopric chose to be silent and focus its sermons on a less thorny subject, the social costs of Menem's economic policies.

The pages of the newspapers, radio and television programs, and the forums of Argentines who live outside the country and communicate with each other over the Internet were overflowing with dialogues and reflections on the reappearance of the taboo subject of Argentina's contemporary history. The practice of making people disappear leads to an indefinite torture for their families, whose pain is suspended in time. About a hundred children of the disappeared formed a new human rights organization, the first to be made up of descendants of the victims of the dirty war. Mothers who had encapsulated their pain in reproaches against their children's militancy decided for the first time to find out what had happened to them. Siblings separated after the disappearance or death of their parents met again and told how they had gotten through the years of negation and secrecy.

But the renewed candor to which the society was abandoning itself also needed judicial approbation. Invoking cultural patterns going back to the Stone Age, Sophocles' *Antigone*, and domestic and international law, various family members of disappeared people asked the judiciary to declare a right to truth and to mourning and an obligation to respect the human body. Emilio Mignone, a signatory to one of these presentations, maintained that this had been part of humanity's cultural patrimony ever since Neanderthal man was buried in a cave on a bed of pine branches and covered with a blanket of flowers. He added that archaeologists and anthropologists recognize in the cult of the dead a sign of humanization that is even more significant than the use of tools and fire. "It is through ritual that death enters the symbolic field, and such symbols are precisely what distinguish us from the rest of the animal kingdom. Those who would deny us the right to bury our dead do nothing less than deny our human condition." On the basis of the official records, he continued, the armed forces should inform each family of the fate of its disappeared member. And that information would also serve "as an official acknowledge of the actions taken by the terrorism of the state."

Thus began a new bout of political arm wrestling. The Federal Chamber in Buenos Aires, which ten years earlier had condemned Videla, Massera and the others, recognized the rights that were invoked, declared that the state had an obligation to reconstruct the past and reveal the reality of what took place during the dirty war, and requested from the minister of defense and the chiefs of staff of the army and navy all the information they possessed on the ultimate fate of the disappeared. Under the pretext of the time that had gone by, all of them answered that when they assumed their posts they had found no records. The chamber then ordered them to reconstruct the lists of the disappeared. The staffs answered that they had no means of doing so. But the army established an office to receive any testimony its personnel might voluntarily wish to offer, in strictest confidence, since the Argentine Constitution prescribes that no one is obliged to testify against himself. The navy, however, questioned the right of the judiciary to give such an order, basing its argument on the division of powers, and said that because of the law of Due Obedience and the pardons, "there is no public action. Let forgetfulness, silence, and forgiveness reign over past events."

However, the armed forces did not remain outside the whirl-
wind of passions Scilingo had aroused. Two decades later, a new
generation of young men and women who are now about twenty
years old was embarking on its life, and not only among the families of the victims. At the dinner tables of military families, children
asked their parents what they had done during the dirty war. Some
of them decided to talk about it outside of their homes as well. The
public emotion was so intense that even some news organizations
of very long-established conservative tradition, which had supported the military's actions during the dictatorship, picked up the
testimony of their horrors and competed for the scoop.

Suffering from a depression diagnosed by psychiatrists at the
Military Hospital, discharged after an incident involving an officer, and unemployed, Sergeant Víctor Ibáñez told the hundred-
year-old Buenos Aires morning paper *La Prensa* that airplanes
and helicopters had also taken off from the first garrison of the
army in Buenos Aires with cargoes of political prisoners who
were thrown into the sea from low altitude flights. The noncommissioned officers Federico Talavera, of the police, and Pedro
Caraballo, of the army, also described to the press in detail the
atrocities they saw or committed. Ibáñez was the only one
among them who could positively identify half a dozen victims
and ask their families for forgiveness. In painful dialogues that
the country followed with bated breath through the media, the
father of a disappeared teenager told Ibáñez he would never forgive him, another father thanked him for having brought an end
to nineteen years of mourning without a tomb, and a mother
asked him for information about her son but refused to participate in dialogue with a murderer.

In another news item, General Albano Harguindeguy, a former minister of the interior during the dictatorship, admitted for
the first time that the method of murder without law or trial had
been institutionally decided upon by the high commands of the
armed forces.

The chief of staff of the army, Martín Balza, decided that his turn had come. Stationed outside the country during the worst years of the dirty war, he appeared on television and freely admitted that the army "took power by abandoning the path of constitutional legitimacy," that it went outside the law to fight the guerrilla movement, and that "it unleashed a repression that makes us shudder today." When he began to deliver his mea culpa, he seemed to have read Cortázar's words; he was in favor of "initiating a painful dialogue about the past that was never sustained and that acts like a ghost within the collective consciousness of the country, always returning from the shadows where it occasionally hides." He said that the responsibility lay with the military leadership, a statement that set aside for good the indefensible myth of excesses or mistakes on the part of the lower ranks, and he implied that criminal forms of conduct were ordered vertically through the chain of command. "Priority was given to combatting the adversary on an individualized basis, in some cases locating individual adversaries by obtaining information through illegitimate methods that were beneath dignity, even going so far as to take lives," he added.

The central paragraph of his message postulates a new concept of command and obedience, at a distance both from the stale doctrine of national security and from that of due obedience promoted by former president Raúl Alfonsín. Balza placed the Argentine army in line with those of the countries of the West: "No one is obliged to carry out an immoral order or one at odds with the law and military regulations. Whoever does so commits a criminal act, deserving of the penalty its seriousness merits. Without euphemisms I clearly declare: whoever violates the National Constitution is committing a crime, whoever gives immoral orders is committing a crime, whoever executes immoral orders is committing a crime, whoever employs unjust means to achieve an end he considers just is committing a crime," he said. The journalist on whose program he read his statement asked him if he had consulted with the president. "No," was his laconic response.

In the newly sensitized climate of social catharsis that followed Scilingo's confession, the television appearance of a general who, instead of reciting commonplaces in a threatening tone like his predecessors, humbly acknowledged the atrocities of the past, received a very warm reception. With the election two weeks away, Menem noticed this sudden change in public feeling toward the armed forces and tried to capitalize on it. He called an urgent press conference in which he said that Balza had spoken at his suggestion. In a 180-degree turnaround, he added that this should be taken into account when the time came to vote. After forty-five days of denying the facts and casting aspersions on those who were describing them, the government launched a huge drive to take advantage of them and ordered the chiefs of staff of the other two armed forces to perform a public self-criticism as well, an order that was reluctantly obeyed by the air force and the navy. Air Force General Juan Paulik admitted that "errors and horrors" had been committed, and Admiral Molina Pico acknowledged that until then the navy had lied about the facts, hiding its use of "a methodology that did not respect the prevailing legal order and the laws of war. These were mistaken methods which gave rise to horrors that were unacceptable even in the cruel context of war. For that reason, we reject them today and we exclude them as a possibility in any future action whatsoever."

Chapter Sixteen
Breaking the Shell

OFTEN IN human history, great secrets are revealed by a solitary conscience, in this case that of a man who slowly freed himself from institutional servitude. When Scilingo lost his balance and was about to fall into the sea together with one of his victims, the military mechanism of depersonalization and dehumanization broke down inside him. For the first time he was able to see the enemy as a human being. Years later, he entered a definitive state of crisis because of his superiors' evasive stance. The military architecture, which tends toward the efficiency of the whole to the detriment of individual liberty, comes crashing down if those who give the orders do not take responsibility for their consequences.

Nevertheless, Scilingo's discourse remained confused. Neither the collective tragedy in which he played a part, the devastating effect it had on his personal life, nor the decision that, to his credit, led him to make a public confession, automatically brought any lucidity to his reasoning. He was overwhelmed with guilt, yet exonerated the dirty war which in his own words made him into a murderer, and he demanded indulgence for those who had only been carrying out orders. But even Thomas Aquinas (the patron saint of Latin American conservatives) wondered in his *Summa Theologica* if the man who performs a guilty act out of obedience is innocent. And he gave as an example the military subordinate. He answers with no doubt whatsoever that the dictates of one's personal conscience can never be violated. If a superior orders one to say that God does not exist or to insult one's mother, one must disobey or resign from one's position — not two decades later, when one has been destroyed by the consequences of one's actions, but at the very moment of receiving the order.

It isn't only Argentine society that is changing. Scilingo, too, looks like a different man, shaken by the social reaction to his confession.

"President Menem began by discrediting you as a scoundrel..."

"I'm talking about tremendous things that happened in this country, and they give these idiotic responses."

"Then he claimed that your accusation wasn't serious because you didn't identify the victims."

"I already clearly explained that I don't know the identity of the people I threw into the sea. I received a group of prisoners with the order to take them on two flights, but since I wasn't in the intelligence section I didn't know who they were. I'm the first person who's interested in identifying them."

"Finally, he said you should only be talking to your confessor."

"If only things were as easy as that! I already confessed. I talked to a priest at the School immediately after the first flight, and it didn't help me at all. I can't accept that what we did can be justified with biblical parables. No Catholic can say that the story ends once I've confessed. If only everything could be resolved in the confessional."

"Confession may give some individual relief, but there's also a social dimension to this issue."

"Yes. And the president has taken this as a personal problem of mine. No one should talk any more about Scilingo. Though it may be a little egotistical to say so, my public confession has brought me a certain relief. Before, I had a secret I couldn't talk about to anyone. Now I can talk to everyone. But the problem still exists."

"Menem also said that this was an electoral issue."

"Please, it's been ten years at least that I've been trying to talk about this. What's more—who's going to benefit from this in the elections? I'm thinking of voting for Menem, although I'm hurt by his lack of understanding."

"Why are you going to vote for him?"

"As a man he doesn't understand, but that doesn't disqualify him as a head of state. I think that the balance of these past six years is positive."

"What seems positive to you?"

"Basically, the economic stability."

"And the pardon?"

"The president's intentions were good: to close a very painful chapter in our history and reconcile the country. But today it seems to me that all of us who committed those barbaric acts should be in prison. I know it's a little irresponsible to say so now, after the Full Stop law which made that impossible. So we could offer up a true, permanent mea culpa and pay our debt. And the most important effect of that would be on those who remained in the institution, people who are new or who didn't get their hands dirty. It would help them to reflect, as a reminder of what they must not do. The president should order the chief of staff of the navy to inform the country of everything that happened during those years, to give out the list of the disappeared. It did me good to speak, it would also do the society good, and it would do the navy good. Especially the new generations of the military, so they don't continue to bear the stigma of ESMA. Otherwise we can't be sure these things won't happen again some time."

"You say that you feel good now?"

"No. I say that it did me good to speak, that I feel better. But I don't feel good. I'm going to feel bad for as long as I live. This is something that can't be overcome."

"The lists of the disappeared are already known. What is not known are the circumstances under which each victim was kidnapped, the treatment they were given, how they were killed."

"Of course. The lists are known by the families of those who are no longer here and the organizations that compiled them. That's why I say that it's the navy that must give the information. All those who were killed by the subversives are buried, and their families know where. On the other side, no. I've often gone to the Plaza de Mayo, like an idiot, like a coward, hiding behind the trees, to watch the Mothers walking around the plaza on behalf of the disappeared, knowing that I had thirty disappeared people on my conscience."

"During our first conversations, you said that your goal was to save the careers of Pernías, Rolón, and Astiz."

"Yes. I told you that if they promoted others who did the same as they did, it was unjust that they were denied promotion."

"That was a petty and unacceptable motive. No self-respecting democracy can give the green light for kidnappers, torturers, and murderers to reach the top of the pyramid, only because others were promoted before them."

"I used to think that, but I realize that it was a pretext I needed to give myself in order to make the decision to speak. When I told what I had done, something much more important opened up. Remember how I always referred to the methods that were ordered for detaining, interrogating, and eliminating the enemy. It was hard for me to say it in other words."

"What other words?"

"Kidnapping, torturing, murdering."

"And now you can?"

"I just said them. When I started to talk, my state of mind was still very closed. Before every interview I took a tranquilizer and worked myself into a tough mind-set. I was afraid someone would see me cry, because that didn't seem fitting for a military man. That's why I said that we had won the war, and that confused some people. Someone told me that my position seemed contradictory, that he didn't understand if I regretted what I had done or not."

"*What was your response?*"

"At that time I was convinced we were doing the right thing. There are people who would rather have a romance novel, who would rather that I say they forced me to do it, that it was against my will or my beliefs. Now almost twenty years have gone by. Of course I have repented. More than that, I'm destroyed by what I did. But I've begun to break the military shell. If I have tears in my eyes I'm not worried that someone might see them. Not only am I feeling like a human being, I'm also beginning to think like an ordinary person. What's more, this has changed my family life. There are things I told you that I hadn't talked about even with my wife. I almost didn't talk to my children at all. Now we talk every day. And at those moments it makes an impression on me all over again that we could have done what we did."

"*I'll repeat a question you weren't able to answer before. How was it possible that none of you realized what you were doing at that time?*"

"You said we were indoctrinated. That could be. But I think that explanation is insufficient. The only answer is that we were in a state of insanity, we were demented. And I'm not forgetting about the things that the subversive movement was doing, the bombs and the assassinations. But we were an armed force, and we should have acted differently. We could have acted differently."

"*What reaction have you had from civilians?*"

"I try not to appear in public too much, because I didn't do

what I did so I could be proud of myself or be praised. What will
they do next, make me into a hero? I'm no kind of hero. But people who have recognized me in the street have told me to keep
doing what I'm doing, not to soften my stance."

"What does that mean?"

"I asked one of them. He told me to keep on with my crusade
to establish the truth. I told him that what I was doing wasn't a
crusade. If I spoke out it was because I couldn't stand myself
anymore. But I know that happens to a lot of people in the
armed forces and it happens to the armed forces themselves as
an institution."

*"Why after almost twenty years are you the only one who
is talking?"*

"I talked because I felt tormented. And most of those who
went through ESMA or the flights must be tormented. They
must have the same struggle I have, to talk or not to talk. I
don't think there is a human being alive who would be capable of keeping this secret for life. Maybe in the future they
won't talk publicly, but at least they'll have to tell their wives
about it."

An idea strikes him and makes him change roles. Now he's the
one who asks:

"Did I tell you that my sister was with the Montoneros?"

"Never."

"She was a member of the group at the university. With paper,
not weapons. She was noble and idealistic. We argued a lot.
She made fun of me, told me I didn't understand anything. I tried
to convince her to leave the group. She didn't pay any attention
to me and kept on. Fortunately nothing happened to her.
Afterward we became very good friends, more than just brother
and sister."

"And now?"

"She died of cancer at age forty-two."

When he evokes her memory he smiles beatifically, as if he

were still incapable of imagining an encounter between the anonymous victim and the bureaucrat of death aboard a coast guard Skyvan or a navy Electra.

Epilogue

MENEM WAS reelected president, and from Juan and Evita Perón's famous balcony he vented his deepest feelings: "We have triumphed not only over the opposing parties, but also over the press."

His government pressured the Federal Chamber until four of its six judges declared that the laws and decrees protecting the military from prosecution obliged them to close the cases without any further investigation. Official obligation to cast light upon the fate of the disappeared was delegated to the undersecretary of human rights, an office of the Executive Power, which considers the payment of indemnities to be answer enough for the long-suffering family members of the disappeared. It was made clear that the settlement of accounts with a shadowy past would have to be done, like so many other things, without intervention from the state.

Massera, the former admiral, was quoted in a news article in which he denied the facts once more. His statements met with unanimous repudiation, even from the chief of staff of the navy. Admiral Molina Pico said in contrast that under Massera's leadership the navy had kidnapped, tortured, and murdered prisoners.

In the meantime, Scilingo was accused of the crime of fraud and arrested. From jail, he sent letters to the judiciary with information about a priest and a pregnant woman who were held at ESMA and with suggestions on how to continue the investigation of the disappeared.

Afterword

AGENTS OF state-sponsored terrorism sometimes break the code of silence that links them to their accomplices and comrades and tell their stories. When they do, as Lieutenant Commander Adolfo Scilingo does in this book, the societies in which they live and to which they speak are shaken by contradictory reactions. It is naturally very difficult to separate the enormity of the crimes they describe from our reflection on their own guilt in them. Certainly, the fact that they speak out—especially when they can safely do so without facing prosecution—does not relieve them of their moral responsibility. But the weight of their testimony as participants and the glimpses that they offer into the horror that is part of the experience of most of their fellow citizens stun the society into a new awareness and transform the discourse about national priorities almost instantly.

Unfortunately, these confessions do not happen often enough. Repressive bodies have a remarkable capacity to prolong the secrecy of their operations years and decades after their end and long after those forces have seen their power and influence in society dwindle. Within the select community of their members, an implicit covenant of silence prolongs the complicity between planners, supervisors, and commanders and subordinates, perpetrators, and executioners. The decision to speak out under those circumstances does set Scilingo and precious few others apart from those who committed the crimes and now continue to injure their victims and society by keeping those crimes secret.

Secrecy and deniability (not altogether "plausible" in this case, given the scale of the crimes) were key to the tactics of "disappearances," the technique overwhelmingly favored by the Argentine military dictatorship of 1976-83. Special "task forces" set up within the chain of command abducted their targets at home, at work, or in the streets and took them to clandestine detention centers where they subjected them to extreme forms of physical and psychological torture. Their tormentors were deliberately shielded from any possible inquiry by a judicial or other authority. When the task forces obtained all the intelligence they needed, the majority of the victims were murdered and their remains disposed of in a variety of ways. The method preferred by the navy was to throw them, while still alive, from transport aircraft into the waters of the Río de la Plata or of the Atlantic Ocean, as Scilingo describes.

For its effectiveness in the "war against subversion," the tactic of disappearances depended heavily on secrecy. Uncertainty about the fate of those abducted sowed terror in society, forced friends and relatives to renounce and ignore old ties, intimidated parents and siblings into not denouncing their plight for fear of making matters worse for their loved ones, and allowed pillars of society, who might otherwise have raised their voices in protest, to pretend they did not know what was going on. Uncertainty is the hardest blow leveled at parents, spouses, and children, and it victimizes them for the alleged sins of their child, spouse, or parent. Even when it becomes clear that their loved one is gone forever, the lack of a body, a grave, or even some information about the circumstances of the death renders them unable to turn their grief into mourning and get on with their lives.

Disappearances, then, are a "continuing offense" and not only or strictly in legal terms. For as long as the uncertainty remains, they are an open wound in the fabric of society that is not healed by amnesty laws or clemency decrees and much less by lofty calls to "reconciliation" lamely uttered from time to time by political or religious leaders. Without public acknowledgment, reconciliation is an empty gesture, or worse, another name for impunity. Victims are asked to reconcile themselves with the torturers and the murderers while the latter are not even asked to atone for their sins by telling the families what they know. And when the families insist on knowing the whole truth, they are perversely accused by self-styled opinion makers of vindictiveness and of being stuck in the past. Fortunately, the majority of the Argentine public agrees with the families of the disappeared that true reconciliation can come only after the whole truth is known.

To be sure, Argentina has done more to restore truth and justice in the aftermath of the "dirty war" than most other countries in similar circumstances. As democracy returned, in 1983, President Raul Alfonsín and the new Congress annulled a shameless amnesty that the military had decreed for themselves in the waning hours of their reign. A blue ribbon panel, chaired by the writer Ernesto Sábato, was created to inquire into the phenomenon of disappearances. The president ordered the prosecution of the members of the successive juntas that had governed the country since 1976 for their responsibility in massive violations of human rights. Congress enacted amendments to the Code of Military Justice that set the stage for prosecutions of all cases of arbitrary arrest, kidnapping, murder, and torture committed by state agents.

In the next two years, the country learned a great deal about the monstrous machinery of repression installed by the military. The Sábato Commission's report, entitled *Nunca Más* (Never Again) and released in late 1984, pointed out the use of more than 250 clandestine detention and torture centers, described some of the abject forms of torture used to extract confessions or information, and documented the deliberate policy of misappropriating children of "disappeared" parents and of murdering captive mothers only after they gave birth, so that babies born in captivity could be given out in illegal adoption. Later, the trial of the junta members further documented these atrocities and provided irrefutable evidence of the existence of a master plan devised by the high command to treat the problem of subversion in this fashion. With the persuasive power of a civilian court acting in open trial and with the majesty of justice, the Argentine public learned that high-ranking military leaders had made themselves "lords of life and death" over thousands of citizens and had proceeded meticulously to supervise through the chain of command the day-to-day operations of their killing machine.

Against the wishes of President Alfonsín, the conviction of former junta members (including two former presidents, Generals Jorge Videla and Roberto Viola) created only the expectation and the demand for more justice. Generals who had been chiefs of security zones or their subdivisions or heads of police forces during the dirty war were in the dock next. They would be prosecuted and tried, also in open trials and before civilian courts, together with their subordinates, many of whom were still on active duty in the armed and security forces. At this point, President Alfonsín allowed democracy to be blackmailed. Succumbing to pressure from the military, he attempted to restrict the normal course of justice through the law of *Punto Final* (Full Stop), which set very short terms within which all charges had to be brought. The tactic backfired: sixty days later, in a rush to beat the deadline, around 450 known suspects had been arraigned.

The military then turned the pressure up: at Easter-time 1987, a faction of the army infantry popularly known as *carapintadas* (because of their use of black camouflage on their faces) rebelled and demanded an end to the prosecutions. Alfonsín then forced through Congress the Due Obedience law, by which all officers (except those who were chiefs of security areas and zones or chiefs of police forces) were presumed irrebuttably to have acted in ignorance of the illegality of the orders they had received. Despite its legal, moral, and factual absurdity, the Due Obedience law's effect was impunity for hundreds of perpetrators. The handful of high-ranking officers who might still have been prosecuted were pardoned by Alfonsín's successor, Carlos Saúl Menem, in 1989. In December 1990, Menem completed the cycle of impunity by pardoning those who had been convicted in the only two cases that reached the sentencing stage.

The obligation of a state to account for the human rights violations of a recent past has several dimensions. Impunity must be overcome by a deliberate attempt to investigate, prosecute, and punish the abusers. The facts thus uncovered must be disclosed to the victims and their relatives, and to society as well. Even if punishment is unavailable, the authorities have a duty to ensure that the ranks of the armed and security forces of a democratic state do not include anyone who has committed atrocities. The state also owes to the affected families a measure of reparation that is consistent with the enormity of the wrong they suffered and also respects their dignity.

In that light, the balance sheet of the extraordinary Argentine experience is as follows: As for justice, there is now no judicial redress available to the victims and their relatives to seek prosecution of the perpetrators. On the other hand, General Videla and Admiral Eduardo Massera were each sentenced to life and actually served seven or eight years in a military jail. Three fellow junta members and General Ramon Camps, the notorious chief of police of the Province of Buenos Aires, also served time in prison. The time served is painfully small in comparison with the enormity of their crimes, but it is nonetheless an important milestone in reasserting the rule of law and erasing the unwritten privilege so often granted to criminal defendants only because they wear uniforms. Hundreds of known torturers are free from prosecution and even free from civil actions for damages. But many of them are well-known to the public, and if the state must consider them innocent by operation of the laws and decrees of impunity, society frequently makes clear that their crimes are not forgotten. Whenever they venture into the streets or public places, Videla, Massera, Camps, and several others have experienced spontaneous though nonviolent acts of repudiation: waiters refuse to serve them, other patrons leave the place or sit far away from them, some actually defy their bodyguards and confront them with the opinion that most Argentines have of them. (This is also true, by the way, of former guerrilla leaders who led so many young Argentines into an aimless, deadly "war," and later shamelessly grabbed Menem's pardon, thereby putting themselves in the same category as Videla et al.)

The democratic administrations have done nothing to force the known torturers into retirement. Lamely citing a misguided version of the presumption of innocence, civilian leaders have resisted calls for disciplinary removal of known criminals or for administrative ends to their careers on the basis of the judicial records. For more than a decade, notorious criminals like navy Commander Alfredo Astiz rose quietly through the ranks. Indeed, this "let sleeping dogs lie" approach may have contributed to early instability of democracy by sending the message that *all* members of the armed forces were suspect, regardless of the existence of evidence of abuse against them. Fortunately, Argentine law specifies that promotion to the rank of colonel or its equivalent (in the navy, the rank of captain) requires the Senate's consent. Accordingly, each time an annual petition to the Senate from the Defense Ministry has included the names of well-known "task force" members, public outcry has forced the Senate to reject them, or the executive branch to withdraw their names in embarrassment. The controversy surrounding the eventually failed promotion of navy officers Pernías and Rolón, carefully described by Verbitsky in this book, seems to have been the final straw that promoted Scilingo's decision to go public. Here, also, the public's refusal to forgive and forget substitutes for the moral cowardice of democratic leaders who hope that these things will simply go away if we continue business as usual—though, in these matters, in the dark if at all possible.

On reparations, the Menem administration deserves credit. Most claims against the state were barred by the Civil Code's very short statute of limitations (two years) and by the courts' unwillingness to consider it interrupted during the dictatorial years. Claims against individual perpetrators were made impossible by the lack of a preliminary finding of criminal liability. When Argentina was brought before the Inter-American Commission on Human Rights, the government settled with some seventy plaintiffs who had been held for years in administrative detention without trial. Then the Congress, at Menem's initiative, passed a law that provides generous reparations to about eight thousand persons held in those years under state-of-siege powers. More recently, Congress extended the reparations scheme to the families of the disappeared, acknowledging the wrong committed by the state against them and not asking the families to endure the indignity of equating their cases to those "presumed dead" because they abandoned their families and are still absent after seven years.

With respect to truth, the Sábato report and the records of the junta trial have uncovered vast documentation about the master plan and its execution. The two pseudoamnesty laws and Menem's pardons have prevented the courts from discovering further details about the role of each cog in the wheel of repression. The preliminary inquiries conducted in hundreds of pretrial investigations, however, provide a wealth of information that is available to the public and has been widely covered in the Argentine press, even though the evidence cannot be put to the test of cross-examination. But neither Alfonsín nor Menem has done anything to pursue the many leads that these sources provide.

The Sábato Commission compiled individual files for around nine thousand cases. At the end of its work, the files were placed in the custody of the Under-Secretariat of Human Rights at the Ministry of Interior. Since then, little has been done to update and enrich those records with those kept by the courts, for example. When nongovernmental organizations have sought to consult them in order to help families achieve some closure to their grief, they have not received adequate cooperation. Indeed, an exceptional group of young professionals called the Argentine Team for Forensic Anthropology made stunning identifications and cause-of-death determinations in a few cases, but found little official cooperation when they attempted to identify hundreds of remains found in unmarked graves. Sadly, the Argentine forensic anthropologists are more in demand around the world than in their own country. At some point early in Menem's term, plans were drafted at the human rights office of the Ministry of Interior to follow through on the records of the Sabato Commission, to establish the ultimate fate of each disappeared person using forensic technology where appropriate, and to provide each family with the information that could be reliably established. Such plans were not approved by the Menem administration, and they have now been abandoned.

The result is that, twenty years later, more than nine thousand Argentine families still do not know exactly what happened to the person who was once yanked away from his or her home by agents of the state, never to be seen again. At the time, the military authorities told them they could not know and would never know. Now, democratically elected leaders and their sycophants in politics, religion, and the media tell them that they should not want to know.

The public debate that followed the Argentine publication of *The Flight* (*El Vuelo*) in March 1995 (which is described in this English version) showed that the majority of Argentines instantly recognized that the state still owes the families more than money, recognition, and a general report: they have a right to know all that can be fairly established about the fate of their loved ones, including the circumstances of their deaths, the identity of their victimizers, and the location of their remains. Reconciliation can come only after the state lives up to this duty.

This book has done much to put this unfinished business on the national agenda. In 1995, the courts ordered the armed forces to produce records and lists of the disappeared. As of this writing, the administration has refused and the matter is sitting at the Supreme Court, a majority of whose members are hopelessly subservient to Menem. The relatives of the disappeared are lobbying Congress for the creation of a commission of inquiry to complete the Sábato Commission's task. It will not be easy. Menem chooses to attack the messenger rather than to heed the unmistakable message. The commander of the navy—who has a close relative counted among the disappeared—continues to think that his task is to defend the honor of his force by denying the obvious and publicly defending the "moral qualities" of officers who escaped prosecution only because of the Due Obedience law. Neither he nor the chief of the air force have come close to the stunning honesty and dignity of General Balza's apology to the nation for the crimes committed by the army during the dirty war.

It seems true that Balza's leadership of the army goes beyond his historic speech of April 25, 1995. One hopes his initiatives will turn the army into the loyal subordinate of democratic authority that it has not been since 1930. One aspect of his now famous speech, however, remains unfulfilled. Balza called on all officers who have knowledge of the events of the dirty war to come to him voluntarily, under promise of confidentiality, so that he could in turn disclose to the families whatever information might be reported about specific victims and incidents. Significantly, not a single officer has come forward. In this part of his speech, General Balza was wrong: he should not have asked for cooperation; he should have ordered his subordinates to produce it as a matter of military discipline and as state agents who are duty-bound to assist the administration in fulfilling its obligations to the citizenry. It makes no sense to allege that such an order would violate the officers' right against self-incrimination, since no criminal prosecution is possible at this stage anyway.

If Scilingo's revelation created such a stir in public discourse, dominating the political agenda for months, why has it failed to prompt other officers into imitating him? The immediate answer is that the public pillorying he received from his superiors, including comments on his moral character and his sanity, must have discouraged anyone who might have been thinking of coming forward. In an attempt to silence potential imitators, Menem even toyed with the legally absurd idea of repealing the Due Obedience law, as if immunity from prosecution had been a factor in Scilingo's candor. But there has to be a more profound reason for the obstinate silence of the "dirty warriors."

Despite the consolidation of democracy in Latin America, military establishments still consider themselves a caste above society and not subject to the rule of law. They believe themselves "protectors of the nation" not so much against external aggression as against the enemy within. "The nation" for them is an abstract term, a spiritual concept that is permanent, while the constitution, democracy, or any other form of government is strictly contingent. In this conceit, their fellow citizens, including those prone from time to time to support them, are held in contempt. This ideology has so permeated the mindset of the officer corps that they and their families lead their lives in isolation from the people they are supposed to serve.

It was not always like this. In most of Latin America, armies were created under the liberal and progressive ideals of the nineteenth century, as the "people in arms." In this century, however, they became the tool of the conservative forces that could no longer get elected by fairly playing by the rules of the democratic game. In the case of Argentina, from this early subordinate position in 1930, through successive coups d'etat and pressuring of weak civilian governments, the military adopted a more autonomous, self-directed ideology, coming to be known at times as "the military party," exercising authority over and no longer serving economic, social, or political forces. Not coincidentally, the "enemy within" was defined in terms of the party that had the clearest chance of winning in democratic elections: in the 1930s it was the *radicales* and, to a lesser extent, the fledgling Socialist Party. In 1955 and thereafter, the main object was to prevent the *peronistas* from bringing back their leader from exile. In the late 60s and 70s, when a generation of Argentines who had never been allowed to vote seemed to embrace the winds of radical change then sweeping most of the world, the enemy was the dangerous amalgam of Peronist populism and revolutionary socialism.

This spiral of increasingly violent confrontation corresponds neatly with the military's turn toward intolerance and authoritarianism, and with the progressive abandonment of legal or ethical limitations in the methods of repression. At first, successful coup leaders formed "provisional" governments and called for new, tutored elections in a reasonably short time. In 1966, General Onganía announced that his regime would last twenty years. In 1976, Videla insisted that his government had goals, not deadlines. Torture has been used since 1930; but repression was highly selective at first. Arbitrary execution of political enemies was committed—for the first time in the century—against Peronist plotters in 1956. And yet, before 1976, repression, while brutal, was highly selective, and some forms of judicial supervision were nominally observed. In contrast, the Videla regime multiplied tenfold the highest number of political prisoners ever held before and embarked on the deadly, methodical, cruel tactic of disappearances. Needless to say, selectivity was replaced by a grotesque witch hunt of young men and women labeled "subversive" for their left-leaning ideas or for their social work among the poor. Explicitly, the definition of subversive went way beyond the armed guerrilla to include lawyers, priests, teachers, artists, labor activists, neighborhood organizers, students, and their friends and acquaintances.

In this climate, the military leaders did not need to persuade their cadres to engage in their barbarous acts. There were precious few who refused to obey manifestly illegal orders, and they were forced into early retirement. Membership in the "task forces" was a career opportunity and a chance to wield influence over and above rank. But while the crimes may have been committed by a small minority of the forces and ordered and supervised by a discrete chain of command going all the way to the top. The rest certainly consented peacefully and explicitly supported the strategy.

After the crushing defeat in the Falklands-Malvinas war, the military was unable to prevent the advent of democracy or even to place too many conditions on the new government. But the successive commanders acting under Alfonsín and Menem were determined to limit the damage. The subordinates who might face prosecution were persuaded to remain silent and trust their leaders' ability to immunize them through pressures on the government. The strategy succeeded: not one piece of the massive evidence gathered by the National Commission on the Disappeared or by courts and prosecutors was obtained through the cooperation of the military, officially or unofficially rendered. Even after the pardons this "covenant of silence" has remained in effect, perhaps because the high command speculates that public opinion is fickle and will one day come to see all this evidence as false.

In the meantime, a curious tension develops within the ranks: the high command insists on silence, while the named perpetrators of the crimes remain identified in the public's consciousness as torturers and murderers. The latter feel, not without reason, that their superiors are letting them hang out to dry as moral scapegoats. If Commander Molina Pico pretends that "the navy" did nothing wrong, then the image he intends to plant in the public mind is that the crimes of the infamous ESMA camp were committed by a small band of rogue elements operating on their own. If it weren't for the report and for the trials of the mid-1980s, this perverse tactic might work. As it is, there is too much knowledge in the public domain to be ignored or to be explained away with inane abstractions.

Under these circumstances, this covenant of silence looks a lot less like loyalty and esprit de corps and more like the Mafia code of *omertà*. This code is not enforced by threat of death, but—just as in criminal organizations—it originates in each party's link to the crimes committed jointly. Scilingo's motivation was not to help the families exercise their right to know, but to expose the fallacy of the navy's pretense that there had never been illegal orders. To his credit, despite his travails after this book was published, he has renewed his pledge to cooperate with any and all attempts to clarify the facts further. There have been others who publicly acknowledged their participation in the crimes of the dirty war, notably Julio Simón (a.k.a. "Julian the Turk") and army Major Héctor Verges. The difference is that these two were widely known to have played important roles in the crimes — at the time of the Due Obedience law Verges was in custody awaiting trial for murder — while Scilingo had never before been named. Also, Simón and Verges expressed no remorse but took to the radio and television microphones in an attempt to sensationalize and trivialize at the same time, exaggerating their own importance and bragging about their continued influence in the intelligence services. Pretty soon they were offering their "files" for money to foreign journalists (without compensation).

Confronted with the grotesque "testimonies" of Verges and Simón, the families and the public are justified in demanding truth with dignity. Instinctively, Scilingo's story is more credible and influential, not only because he could have continued in anonymity, but also because he chose to tell his story to Horacio Verbitsky, Argentina's most successful and respected investigative journalist. Given Verbitsky's record exposing corruption, undue influence over the judiciary, and the dirty war itself, in approaching him Scilingo could not have hoped for a friendly forum. In the public's mind, the fact that he accepted Verbitsky's tough and knowledgeable cross-examination is evidence of Scilingo's good faith. Since the public knows that many of Verbitsky's colleagues are counted among the disappeared (Verbitsky himself lived many years in exile), the interview was all the more stunning as the confession of a task force member made to someone who could very easily have been one of his faceless, nameless victims.

Argentina's experiment with truth and justice is now more than twelve years old. Since then, several other countries have traveled their own roads, and some—such as Haiti and South Africa—are beginning their own. Yet in 1995, Argentina entered into a new phase of the policy debate as a result of this book. The latest twists in the policy of accountability suggested by the issues on the Argentine agenda should prove valuable to the efforts in other countries, just as the historic achievements of the early Alfonsín years informed the transitions in Chile, El Salvador, Haiti, Guatemala, Honduras, and now South Africa, and are present in the international community's effort to bring peace—with justice—in the former Yugoslavia and in Rwanda. From now on, the attitudes of military leaders towards crimes committed by their subordinates will be measured by how they compare to General Martin Balza's apology to the nation; a process of truth-telling will be judged by how much secrecy is shed in telling each victim and each family exactly what happened.

One lesson to be learned is how to encourage those who hold the secrets to come forward. In hindsight, the prospect of prosecutions up and down the chain of command in Argentina may have contributed to the officers' hanging tough together with their superiors. But it is not just a matter of offering immunity to the lower ranks, because that would violate the principle established in Nuremberg that obedience to illegitimate orders is not an excuse. Encouraging the culprits to speak out should not be regarded as equivalent to condoning their crimes. On the contrary, it signals that if reconciliation is the goal, the perpetrators must take the first step by breaking the veil of secrecy that is the first condition of impunity.

In countries not directly affected by the legacy of "dirty wars" there should also be a more enlightened understanding of the value of truth telling as an element of accountability. The United States refuses to release information in its files about paramilitary groups in Haiti, even though some of those files are actually Haitian government property taken by U.S. forces during the recent occupation. That lack of cooperation may well doom the efforts of the fledgling democratic government to restore some measure of truth and justice to the decades of brutality against the poor. Canada denies asylum to Florencio Caballero, a low-ranking member of the notorious Battalion 316 in Honduras, whose escape and testimony before the Inter-American Court of Human Rights was instrumental in revealing the structure that made possible the two hundred disappearances of the early 1980s. Honduras is finally prosecuting some of the Battalion 316 leaders originally identified by Caballero; in contrast, Canada seeks to deport him under an extremely narrow reading of the principle that those who participate in the persecution of others are not entitled to asylum.

Truth telling, however, is only part of the process of accountability. The success of "truth commissions" in several countries has generated a perverse and paradoxical result: those who consider themselves political realists are no longer urging a forgive-and-forget attitude. Instead, they urge the creation of "truth commissions" as a way of leaving a messy past behind as quickly as possible. This has even been proposed for Bosnia, to entice the leaders of the genocide to accept a peace plan in exchange for immunity from prosecution. The recent history shows, however, that truth commissions work only if they are conceived as a key element of accountability, not as a pretext for impunity. A report premised on impunity will, almost by definition, be far from a truthful report. In Bosnia, all that could reasonably be accomplished by a truth commission has been done to exhaustion by various U.N. bodies, in reports that world leaders deliberately refuse to read. Only prosecutions before the International Criminal Tribunal for the Former Yugoslavia can now bring the detailed truths that the victims deserve, through rigorous investigative methodology and validated through trial before an independent judicial body. And if this results in punishment for genocide, peace will be served as well as truth and justice.

Truth, therefore, should not be conceived as an alternative to justice. Argentina's recent example shows that even honest global reports are not enough. A free society demands and deserves to know everything. A free society also understands that it has a duty to offer the victims of human rights abuse a fair exercise of their right to see justice done, and that this right to justice does not consist only of an apology and compensation.

These lessons will soon be tested in different parts of the world. They have not been strong enough to prevent Peru from enacting last year a shameful blanket amnesty for all the crimes committed by military and police forces since 1982, but the Fujimori government did pay an important price in international discredit. In Chile, despite the presence of General Augusto Pinochet still at the head of the army, the newly democratic regime also appointed a Truth and Reconciliation Commission that has produced an exemplary report on the crimes of the Pinochet era. Files and records are made available to families to follow through on every lead to establish the fate and whereabouts of each victim. Pinochet's principal henchman in repression, General Manuel Contreras, and his deputy at the intelligence services have finally been convicted in the murder of former Foreign Minister Letelier in Washington in 1976, the one case not covered by the Junta's self-amnesty law of 1978. And as this prologue is written, the utter contempt of the Chilean military for the public's right to know is being shaken by the capture in Argentina of an intelligence operative long sought for his role in the murder, in Buenos Aires in 1974, of exiled General Carlos Prats. In this case also, Washington is being asked to contribute to justice by making evidence available to courts in Chile and Argentina that so far has remained under the exclusive control of U.S. prosecutors.

All eyes in the human rights community, however, are set now on the new South Africa, where Nelson Mandela has to deal with a legacy of abuse that surpasses anything ever witnessed in Latin America, while maintaining the dream of a multiethnic, reconciled country. His impressive moral authority no doubt is the country's biggest asset in this difficult journey, but clear thinking and respect for moral imperatives have also come from South African civil society. Under a statute enacted in 1995, immunity from prosecution will be conditioned on the suspect coming forward with all he knows, so that the Commission on Truth and Reconciliation headed by Archbishop Desmond Tutu can establish a complete official record of the crimes of the apartheid era. In fact, prosecutions against formerly powerful apartheid leaders have begun; the first case includes a former minister of defense who is currently in custody.

If political realists thought that reconciliation in societies torn by human rights violations might be served by a forgive-and-forget

policy, the stunning developments of the transitions to democracy in Argentina and elsewhere have demonstrated that it is far
better to confront the question of impunity in earnest. It is also
readily apparent that, once a process of accountability is under
way, it is a mistake to try to close it off by pseudoamnesty laws
and pardons. Sooner or later, the families' right to know
the truth is embraced and seconded by the whole society, and
the idea itself becomes so powerful that the state must find
the means to accommodate this legitimate expectation. In
Argentina, that "sooner or later" was the publication of this
book. In ways probably not expected even by its author, in a few
weeks the book renewed the debate about what is owed to the
families of the disappeared. And though the debt is not quite
paid in full, the postpublication events have done much to vindi-
cate the rights of the victims of human rights violations and to
point the way to what needs to be done in other societies strug-
gling to rid themselves of the legacy of cruelty and abuse.

Juan E. Méndez
General Counsel
Human Rights Watch

Sources and Notes

Chapter One: Let's Tell the Truth

The backgrounds of Rolón and Pernías appeared in *Página/12*, December 28, 1993, and October 19, 1994. Testimony concerning Pernías's participation in the case of the French nuns was given to the courts by Ricardo Héctor Coquet, Graciela Daleo, Sara Solarz Osatinsky, Ana María Martí, María Alicia Milia Pirles, and Alberto Girondo. Concerning his involvement with the priests at St. Patrick's, Daleo and Andrés Castillo. Concerning his intention to kidnap the tycoon Julio Broner in Venezuela, Lisandro Raúl Cubas. Concerning Pernías as a teacher of torturers, Amalia Larralde. The prisoner on whom the experiments with the poisoned darts were performed was Daniel Schapira.

Chapter Two: In Praise of Torture

Menem's statement that he had not requested the promotion of the torturers, in *Página/12*, December 29, 1993. Massot on torture, in *Página/12*, January 2, 1994. The debate over torture between Hesayne and Harguindeguy, in the supplement on the pardons in *Página/12*, December 31, 1990. The declaration of Foreign Minister Alain Juppé, in *Clarín*, October 26, 1994. The decision of the Senate Justicialista bloc, in *Página/12*, October 27, 1994. Menem on the triumph of the law, on the radio program *Periodismo y medialunas*, on Radio FM Jai, Tuesday, October 25, 1994. Balza on facing the past with humility, in *La Prensa*, October 27, 1994. On the end and the means, after having become chief of staff, in *Somos*, June 1, 1992 and in his message to new students at the Military College, in *Página/12*, December 17, 1993. The article on Mayorga was written by Jorge Lanata and published in the magazine *El porteño* in April 1985. Mayorga's statements on the injections given to prisoners and his vindication of torture, in Tina Rosenberg's excellent book *The Children of Cain* (New York: William Morrow & Co., 1991), p. 86.

Chapter Three: A Christian Death

In addition to the multitude of testimony on the direct participation of Pernías, Rolón and other navy men in torture sessions, there exists a global analysis of the use of torture during the dirty war. An unpublished study written by one of the surviving ESMA prisoners maintains that each armed force used torture in a different way. The army tried to delegate the use of the electric cattle prod to the police force or to prisoners who had switched sides. The air force performed mystical ceremonies: several officers participated with cattle prods, whips, and sticks, and one of them consoled the victim by taking his or her hand. The navy maintained that in every war there was a decisive weapon that should be reserved for the elite, and compared the electric cattle prod with nuclear arms. For that reason, its use was both a duty and a privilege that was reserved for the officers who were on intelligence duty at ESMA. Only rarely were operative officers such as Astiz or auxiliaries from the security forces permitted to use it. In ESMA's animal phase, the person who used the name "Puma" was Captain Jorge Perren.

Chapter Six: The Institutional Lie

Massera's speech, in *La Nación,* November 3, 1976. Videla's first explanation of the disappeared, in *La Prensa,* September 15, 1977. Viola's calculation of those who were disappeared and killed, in *La Nación,* September 30, 1977. The news article on Massera, in a biography of him by Claudio Uriarte, *Almirante Cero* (Buenos Aires: Planeta, 1992), p. 139. Viola's harangue about those absent forever, in all the Buenos Aires morning papers, May 30, 1979. Harguindeguy's boasts, in *Clarín,* September 22, 1979 and in *La Nación,* March 22, 1980. The warnings by Viola and Galtieri at the time of the changeover in the army, in *Clarín,* April 12, 1980. Also in *Clarín,* on April 17, 1980, Videla's pretensions concerning the legitimacy of the dirty war. The dictatorship's response to the Organization of American States, in *Clarín,* April 20, 1980. The observation that the conservative Francisco Manrique was the only politician concerned with the dirty war was in an interesting declaration by Bignone, in *La Nación,* March 29, 1987. The details on the Church's mediation and the reconciliation mass were provided to me by the leader of the Christian Democratic Party, Augusto Conte. The junta's document to the effect that the political parties had committed themselves not to judge the dirty war, in *Clarín,* November 12, 1982.

Chapter Seven: Boomerang

The cables from ANCLA, the *History of the Dirty War,* and the "Open Letter from a Writer to the Military Junta," in Horacio Verbitsky, *Rodolfo Walsh y la prensa clandestina* (Buenos Aires: Ediciones de la Urraca, 1985).

Chapter Eight: Disinfection

The testimony of the three women who incriminated Pernías in the abduction of the nuns, in the Spanish magazine *La calle,* October 23, 1979. That of Horacio Maggio in the January-March 1979 issue of the magazine *Alternativa,* published in Sweden. Both publications are in the author's personal archive.

Chapter Nine: A Humanist in Uniform

The reform of the Code of Military Justice in the National Chamber of Deputies, *Diario de sesiones,* January 5, 1984, and the National Senate, *Diario de sesiones,* January 31 and February 1, 1984. Massera on the Christian humanism of the dirty war, in his statements before the Supreme Council of the Armed Forces on February 8 and August 30, 1984. Lambruschini on the eradication of cancer, in his declaration to the Supreme Council of the armed forces on February 13, 1984.

Chapter Ten: The Judgment of Mankind

The declarations made by witnesses during the trial are taken from tape recordings of their testimony before the Federal Chamber on April 23 (Admirals Luis María Mendía and Pedro Santamaría), April 25 (Admiral Antoine Sanguinetti), May 2 (Jacobo Timerman), July 4 (Marta Bettini de Devoto), July 16 (priest Orlando Yorio, Captain Oscar Quinteiro), July 17 (former conscript Alejandro Hugo López, Commander Jorge Búsico, and former noncommissioned officer Jorge Torres), July 18 (Graciela Daleo, Miriam Lewin, and Andrés Castillo), and July 25 (Carlos Muñoz), all in 1985. That of Rosario Quiroga from the consular document drawn up in Caracas, Venezuela, on July 13, 1985. The former officer Urien on the teaching of methods of torture, in Rosenberg, *The Children of Cain,* 117.

Chapter Twelve: Modus Operandi

Acosta's declaration of February 27, 1987, is taken from the records of the Federal Chamber and signed by the accused and the judges. The demonstration in the rain in the military zone is described in *La Nación* on February 26 and *La Prensa* on February 27, 1987. The details of the application of the law of escape to three prisoners, as well as the receipt for their withdrawal from the jail, were taken from the case files of the federal court in Córdoba. Astiz's complaint regarding his social isolation, in Rosenberg, *The Children of Cain,* page 134. Juan Yofre on Astiz and Arduino, in *Ambito Financiero,* December 23, 1987.

Chapter Thirteen: Whiskey and Pills
The description of the criminal plan, in the Federal Chamber ruling condemning Videla, Massera, et al., December 1985. The mentions of blind obedience and the respect due the person of the captured enemy, in the ruling of the same court one year later, when it condemned Ramón Camps.

Chapter Fifteen: A Surface Smoothed Down by Death
Molina Pico's radiogram, in *La Prensa,* March 4, 1995. Nuncio Laghi's actions, in *Página/12,* March 9, 11, 12, and 16, 1995. The bishops who acknowledged that the Church did not do enough were Justo Laguna, Carlos Galán, Domingo Castagna, Emilio Bianchi di Carcano, and Jorge Casaretto. Bishop Hesayne on the Conference of Bishops and the Mothers, in *Página/12,* April 16, 1995. The testimony of Sergeant Ibáñez, in *La Prensa,* April 24, 1995. That of Sergeant Caraballo, in *Página/12,* July 1, 1995. The mea culpas of Chiefs of Staff Balza, Molina Pico, and Paulik, in every Buenos Aires newspaper, April 25 and May 4, 1995.

Epilogue
Menem's words about the press, in every Buenos Aires newspaper, May 15, 1995. The decision of the Federal Chamber to close the investigation, in *Página/12,* July 23, 1995. The news article

on Massera, in the magazine *Gente* (no. 1566, July 27, 1995). Molina Pico's response, in the magazine *Noticias*, August 13, 1995, under the title "*Basta de mentiras*" "Enough Lies"). Scilingo's letters from jail, in *Página/12*, July 7 and 9, 1995.

Chronology

1930:

A military coup overthrows President Hipólito Yrigoyen of the centrist party known as the Radical Civic Union. Yrigoyen was the first president to have been cleanly elected by a secret and obligatory vote; he represented the accession to the government of the new middle classes of immigrant origins.

In the following half century, Argentina will undergo no fewer than one military coup per decade and will be governed by more presidents who owe their office to the sword than to the ballot. During this period, which lasted until the democratic election of President Raúl Alfonsín, also a Radical Civic Union member, in 1983, only two elected presidents successfully concluded the constitutional term of six years, and both were retired army generals. One of them, Agustín P. Justo, came to power through fraudulent elections in 1932. The other, Juan D. Perón, was overthrown in the middle of his second term as president in 1955.

1943:

A military group that sympathizes with the Axis Powers takes control of the government. Among them is Perón, then a colonel, who becomes, successively, secretary of labor and social welfare, minister of war and vice president. While serving as secretary of labor he formulates a policy of respect for the rights of workers, inspired by the social doctrines of the Catholic Church.

1945:
Perón is arrested by his comrades and a spontaneous popular demonstration demanding his freedom converges on the center of Buenos Aires from the suburbs.

1946:
Perón is elected president in a clean vote.

1955:
On June 16, navy planes drop nine and a half tons of bombs on the Plaza de Mayo, in front of the Government House, in a failed attempt to overthrow Perón, reelected three years before with 62 percent of the vote. This is the overture to the violence that will envelop Argentina until 1983.

In September, a military junta overthrows Perón, disbands the Congress, dissolves the Supreme Court, takes control of the unions, and governs in a state of siege. A decree by the Executive Power establishes prison sentences for anyone who publicly speaks the name of ex-President Perón or his wife Evita. The military steals Evita's embalmed corpse.

1956:
In June, General Juan José Valle and two dozen Peronists, both military and civilian, are shot on the orders of military president Pedro Aramburu, in reprisal for an uprising aimed at holding free elections.

In October, the exiled Perón sends his "General Directives for all Peronists" and his "Instructions for Leaders," in which he recommends armed resistance against the government, the organization of guerrilla forces to combat it, the use of bombs, and the assassination of adversaries.

Members of the Argentine military take classes at the School of War in Paris while French colonels teach Argentine officers at the military institutes of Buenos Aires. The counterinsurgency tactics employed by the French in Indochina and Algeria are studied.

1958:
Radical Civic Union politician Arturo Frondizi becomes president, elected by the votes of the outlawed Peronist movement, to whom he has promised participation in the country's political system. During the forty-six months of his administration, he will face thirty-two standoffs with the military, some of them involving the deployment of tanks in the streets of Buenos

Aires. The intensity of the Peronist resistance grows; oil pipelines are blown up and there is a generalized sabotage of manufacturing. Striking railroad workers are militarized and soldiers run the trains. Tanks break down the doors of the Lisandro de la Torre meat-packing plant, which has been occupied by its workers.

1959:

On January 1, Fidel Castro and Ernesto Che Guevara enter Havana in triumph. They propose, among other things, to transform the Andes into a larger version of the Sierra Maestra, the mountains where the Cuban insurgency began.

1961:

The Argentine politician John William Cooke, one of Juan D. Perón's personal representatives, participates in the Cuban resistance against the invaders at the Playa Girón in the Bay of Pigs. Cooke invites Perón to relocate to Cuba, but the former president prefers to go to Spain, where he will live until 1973.

U.S. President John F. Kennedy announces the Alliance for Progress. Argentine officers learn counterinsurgency techniques at the School of the Americas, and Argentine guerrillas are trained in Cuba. Superimposed on Argentina's internal political dynamic are the strategic conflicts of the cold war.

1962:

Frondizi allowed Peronist candidates to participate in elections for provincial governorships. One of them wins in the decisive province of Buenos Aires, and as a result Frondizi is overthrown. Strife within the military allows the president of the Senate, José María Guido, rather than the chief of the army, to ascend to the presidency in Frondizi's place. In September, various military factions have an armed confrontation over the control of a weak President Guido.

1963:

In April, the opposing military factions confront each other once more, this time with airplanes and armor-plated vehicles. Army tanks destroy Naval Aviation's runways, giving rise to a lasting hostility. Out of these combats a new strongman emerges, General Juan Carlos Onganía, who presents himself as the leader of the "army of the constitution and the law" and says he supported the call for elections, but then returned to being strictly professional, without intervening in "internal politics." But five weeks after he so clearly stated his submission to the civil authorities, Peronism is outlawed once again. In June, with barely 23 percent of the vote, the Radical Civic Union candidate Arturo Illia is elected president.

1964:

Onganía remains commander in chief of the army. From West Point, he formulates the doctrine of ideological borders and calls for intervention by the army in internal politics as an extraconstitutional watchdog. In Salta, the police break up a Marxist guerrilla detachment.

President Charles de Gaulle of France visits Argentina. Perón orders that he be received as if he were Perón himself, and demonstrations in the streets throughout the country checkmate the government. Months later, Perón attempts to return to Argentina, but, at the request of Illia's government, the Brazilian military detains his plane in Río de Janeiro.

1965:

The Peronists achieve good results in all the elections they are permitted to participate in, which makes them the foreseeable victors of the following year's elections in the province of Buenos Aires.

1966:

On June 28, prior to the provincial elections in Buenos Aires, a military junta overthrows Illia, imposes a Revolutionary Statute that is superior to the Constitution, and installs Onganía in the presidency. The Congress and the Supreme Court are dissolved and all political and labor union activity is banned.

The clerical organization Opus Dei participates in the national cabinet to a significant degree, and Cardinal Antonio Caggiano, who is also a military bishop, signs Onganía's decree of assumption to the presidency and participates in all the official ceremonies. Onganía and a group of prominent generals go on spiritual retreats where they undergo the influence of the Catholic fundamentalist groups Verbe and La Cité Catholique, both of which originated in France.

1968:

A detachment of half a dozen guerrillas, members of the Peronist Armed Forces, is routed in the province of Tucumán.

1969:

On May 29, columns of workers and students occupy Córdoba, the country's second largest city, in protest against Onganía's socioeconomic policies. The police are overwhelmed, and the army intervenes and fires into the crowd in order to regain control of the city. That same day, an unknown guerrilla commando kills Augusto Vandor, leader of the metallurgical workers, who is denounced as a paradigm of the alliance between the Peronist union bureaucracy and the military establishment.

Amid the commotion caused by both episodes, Nelson Rockefeller arrives in Argentina as part of his mission through Latin America. In the report he sends to President Nixon, he describes a growing Communist threat, praises the role of the armed forces, and recommends strengthening the continent's police forces as the first line of combat.

Onganía announces a procession to the sanctuary of Luján in order to consecrate Argentina to the heart of the Virgin Mary. But the Catholic Church is divided: under the auspices of the Second Vatican Council and the meeting of the Latin American Catholic Church in Medellín, many Bishops and priests defend the so-called choice for the poor, justify a violent response to oppression, and support a dialogue between Catholics and Marxists. All the conditions for a militarization of politics are present.

1970:
A commando from the new organization known as the Montoneros, which takes its name from the irregular parties of gauchos who resisted pro-British liberalism during the nineteenth century, kidnaps former dictator Aramburu on May 29. The Montoneros' members emerged from the group known as Catholic Action and participated in social work camps led by priests in the country's poorest regions. The Montoneros combine personal attacks against members of the military and union leaders with community work among the poor and political organizing of the Peronist Youth. After a mock trial for the 1956 shootings, Aramburu is killed in a cellar, and his corpse is submerged in quicklime. From his exile in Madrid, Perón approves of the deed and congratulates the Montoneros, whose first communication commends Aramburu's soul to God.

Onganía is overthrown by the army, which puts in his place the military attaché in Washington, General Roberto Levingston, a counterinsurgency specialist. Massive demonstrations to protest the socioeconomic situation and demand a new political beginning take place across the country, which becomes ungovernable by the military. While the Peronist trade unions are negotiating agreements with the government, a resistance against the military dictatorship is organized by grass roots union leaders, the Montoneros, and the Peronist Youth. The same fracture that had split the Church is now dividing Peronism. Perón says he must act as "The Holy Father" and give his blessing to all the conflicting sectors.

Small Marxist guerrilla organizations known as the "People's Revolutionary army" (ERP) and the "Revolutionary Armed Forces" (FAR) also begin to take action. Both groups are inspired by the Cuban, Chinese, and Vietnamese experiences, but while the ERP remains faithful to Marxist orthodoxy, the FAR begins a process of approximating itself to the mass movement of Peronism.

1971:
The chief of the army, General Alejandro Lanusse, deposes Levingston, assumes the presidency, and calls elections in which, for the first time, the Peronists are permitted to participate. His idea is to strip the guerrillas of their most powerful rallying point and isolate them politically and socially, given the difficulty of suppressing them by force.

1972:
With the help of the Catholic Church, the military had been keeping Evita's embalmed body hidden in a cemetery in Italy; as a gesture of goodwill, Lanusse now returns it to Perón in Madrid. Lanusse passes a law establishing that only those who were residing in the country before August are eligible to be candidates in the upcoming elections and challenges Perón during a meeting of the top ranks of the military: "I don't think he has the guts to come back." Perón returns to Argentina in November, acclaimed by mass demonstrations of hundreds of thousands of people. Since the deadline has passed and he is ineligible to be a candidate, he designates his personal representative, Héctor J. Cámpora, to run for the presidency and returns to Madrid. The campaign's central buzz word is "Cámpora to the government, Perón to power," and the slogan "FAR and the Montoneros are our companions" is chanted at every Peronist rally, which infuriates the military.

On August 22, after faking an escape attempt, the navy executes a dozen guerrillas imprisoned at its base in Trelew. Their bodies are laid out in the central headquarters of the Justicialista Party, but its doors are broken down by the police, who take away the coffins in order to keep the bodies from being autopsied.

1973:
Cámpora is elected president on March 11. For his swearing-in ceremony on May 25, he invites Chilean President Salvador Allende and the Cuban Osvaldo Dorticós. His first decision is to free all the imprisoned guerrillas; this is unanimously approved by Congress, which also dissolves as unconstitutional a special tribunal created to try them. As they arrive from the country's various jails, the prisoners are given a hero's welcome in the provincial government houses. The FAR merges with the Montoneros into a single organization.

On June 20, Perón finally returns to the country. His private secretary and one of Cámpora's ministers, José López Rega, a former chief of police and an astrologer, calls on unionists and members of the military to organize an armed contingent to be positioned on the stage above the crowd gathered near Ezeiza Airport during Perón's first public appearance in Argentina. The crowd begins to assemble the night before and is estimated at more than a million people. When the columns of the Peronist Youth approach, they are fired upon from above. The crowd scatters and at least thirteen people are killed and three hundred wounded by bullets.

Perón comes out against the Montoneros and forces Cámpora to resign. Raúl Lastiri, López Rega's son-in-law, assumes the presidency for an interim period and calls new elections. On September 23, Perón is elected president for the third time, on a ticket completed by his wife Isabelita. Two days later, the Montoneros kill the general secretary of the General Confederation of Labor (CGT), José Rucci, a trade unionist, as one of those responsible for what happened in Ezeiza, but they do not claim responsibility for the attack in order not to enrage Perón. The ERP continues kidnapping U.S. businessmen and demanding ransom for them and attacking army facilities.

1974:

On May 1, Perón calls the Montoneros "immature imbeciles," whereupon they turn their backs on him and leave the Plaza de Mayo half empty. Perón dies on June 1 and Isabelita assumes the presidency, while López Rega governs from behind the throne. The Triple A (Argentine Anti-Communist Alliance) begins to take action, kidnapping and assassinating intellectuals and politicians suspected of links to the guerrillas. In September, the Montoneros announce they are going back underground. The ERP opens a rural guerrilla front in the northern province of Tucumán.

1975:

Without the political umbrella of Peronism, the Montoneros' actions lose their mass character and their acceptance. Isabelita charges the army with controlling the growing social agitation, and Ricardo Balbín, the leader of the opposition party, the Radical Civic Union, says that the striking workers constitute an "industrial guerrilla group." The government orders the army to "annihilate the actions of subversion," first in Tucumán, then throughout the country. The first leader of the troops in Tucumán is General Adel Vilas, a disciple of the French, who defends torture as the weapon of choice in this type of battle and advocates the extension of the conflict to the universities. He is succeeded by General Domingo Bussi, who studied counterinsurgency in Vietnam.

Swept out of Tucumán, the ERP attempts, in the final days of the year, a desperate attack on a Buenos Aires military installation. The attack's failure ultimately leads to the organization's demise. The Montoneros attack a military facility in the province of Formosa, something only the ERP had done until that point, and they are also repelled with heavy losses.

The president of the bishopric, Monseñor Adolfo Tortolo, announces to an audience of business people that a purification process will soon be carried out. The Order for Army Operations includes dispensations for special methods of interrogation, a euphemism for torture. The navy follows suit; the commander of naval operations, Admiral Luis Mendía, communicates this to navy officers in the Puerto Belgrano naval base. He maintains that these methods, as well as the elimination of living prisoners by throwing them into the sea, have been approved by the hierarchy of the Catholic Church. But because of the international isolation of the Chilean dictatorship of Augusto Pinochet, the Argentine military must keep its procedures carefully under wraps.

1976:

On March 23, the commanders in chief of the army, the navy and the air force pay a visit to Monseñor Tortolo at the bishopric's headquarters. Hours later, on March 24, they overthrow and imprison Isabel Perón. The governor of the province of La Rioja, Carlos Menem, and other Peronist leaders, are confined to a navy prison ship anchored in the port of Buenos Aires. Once again, the Congress and the Supreme Court are dissolved. Clandestine concentration camps are set up in units of the armed and security forces, and those who are abducted are taken to them, always secretly and without any judicial order. There they are tortured, then covertly murdered. In a meeting of the bishopric, Tortolo defends torture with theological arguments.

The military junta designates the chief of the army, General Jorge Videla, to be president, but the junta is being torn apart by internal conflicts. Old jealousies are erupting between the army and the navy, led by Admiral Emilio Massera, who maintains that the junta is the organ of maximum power and Videla no more than its delegated administrator.

In the plans approved by the military junta, it falls to the army to command the operations of the dirty war, and the jurisdictions are clearly determined. But Massera does not respect those agreements and invades the jurisdiction of the army as a way of accumulating intramilitary power. His instrument for doing so is the Navy School of Mechanics (ESMA), where a clandestine concentration camp is operating. The task force that administers it answers directly to the chief of the navy, who personally participates in certain operations.

In June, an army patrol brings down the leader of the ERP, Roberto Santucho, and the dismantling of that organization is complete.

Also in June, at a breakfast during a meeting of the Organization of American States (OAS) in Chile, Argentine Foreign Minister Admiral César Guzzetti tells Secretary of State Henry Kissinger what the Argentine military is doing. Kissinger replies that they have to finish off the terrorists before the installation of the new U.S. Congress in January 1977. Kissinger is counting on the reelection of Gerald Ford, who is defeated in November by Jimmy Carter.

1977:

The Argentine military considers Carter's human rights policies a betrayal and establishes links with members of the ultraconservative opposition, such as Senator Jesse Helms. Videla meets with Carter's envoy, Patricia Derian, and tells her he cannot control the lower ranks.

On March 25, the writer and journalist Rodolfo J. Walsh is abducted after having distributed an "Open Letter to the Military Junta," in which he denounced the torture and murder of prisoners.

On Christmas Eve, the members of the founding nucleus of the Mothers of the Plaza de Mayo, which had been infiltrated by Lieutenant Alfredo Astiz, are abducted from the Church of the Holy Cross. They are tortured in the ESMA by Lieutenant Antonio Pernías and never reappear.

1978:

Admiral Massera retires. His successor, Armando Lambruschini, consults with the papal nuncio, Pio Laghi, on the situation of the prisoners. He doesn't want to kill them, but if he leaves them alive he is afraid they will reveal what they saw.

1979:

The Interamerican Commission on Human Rights of the OAS visits Argentina.

1980:

The OAS report appears; it states that the thousands of disappeared persons have been killed by official forces and that the alarming and systematic use of torture has been proven. The government responds that the state is exercising its power of self-defense and using the "appropriate means." Adolfo Pérez Esquivel of the Service of Peace and Justice, who denounces the massive violations of human rights, receives the Nobel Peace Prize.

After Somoza is overthrown by the Sandinistas, the Argentine military trains the first contingents of the Contras, by agreement with the CIA. They also instruct members of the militaries of Honduras, Guatemala, and El Salvador on torture methods.

1981:

A year of economic crisis and a rapid turnover of military presidents. In
March, General Roberto Viola succeeds Videla; in December, General
Leopoldo Galtieri removes Viola from office. The political parties demand
that elections be held for the first time in a decade and the unions demand
economic improvements.

1982:

On April 2, the military junta occupies the Malvinas, Georgias, and South
Sandwich Islands, which have been controlled by Great Britain since the
first decades of the nineteenth century. Margaret Thatcher's government
sends a powerful fleet to recover them. The navy, which had encouraged the
occupation, withdraws its fleet to the coast at the news that the United
Kingdom is using nuclear submarines. Astiz is captured by the British after
surrendering the South Georgias Islands without resistance. Ultimately,
Argentina loses the war. Galtieri is deposed by his peers. Fatally wounded,
the dictatorship calls elections.

1983:

In July, the courts order the arrest of Massera for the murder of a mistress's
husband, the businessman Fernando Branca, who was invited for a sail on
the yacht Massera used as chief of the navy and never appeared.

In September, the military junta passes an autoamnesty for all members
of the military charged with human rights violations. In October the leader
of the Radical Civic Union, Raúl Alfonsín, wins the presidency with 52 percent of the vote; it is the first time the Peronist movement has been defeated
in clean elections. He is sworn into office on December 10. The new Congress nullifies the autoamnesty. Alfonsín creates a presidential commission
of leading members of the society to investigate human rights violations
and asks the courts to press charges against Videla, Massera, and other
leaders of the dirty war.

1984:

At the demand of the national government, which wants the military to purge
itself, the Supreme Council of the Armed Forces orders the arrest of the three
commanders in chief who held power in 1976. The National Commission on
the Disappeared, presided over by the writer Ernesto Sábato, delivers its
report to the president. The report states that human rights were violated in
an institutional and state-ordained manner and that after being tortured the
disappeared were thrown into the river or into the sea. Nine thousand cases
are verified, with the names and surnames of the deceased, but the actual figure is believed to be higher. In a collective response, the Supreme Council

affirms that the orders given by the former commanders were perfectly correct. The Federal Chamber removes the case from the military courts and carries on with the trial, which is extended to include the two military juntas that succeeded the first one. In all, nine former military leaders are charged, three of whom were also de facto presidents.

1985:

Between April and September, the Federal Chamber hears testimony from survivors of the clandestine concentration camps and national and international leaders (such as Patricia Derian) for twelve hours a day. On December 9, Videla and Massera are sentenced to life imprisonment for treasonous homicides, illegal deprivations of liberty, torture, and robbery; former general Roberto Viola, former admiral Armando Lambruschini, and former brigadier general Ramón Agosti all receive prison sentences as well, and all those convicted are also dishonorably discharged from the armed forces.

The sentencing order describes the "criminal plan" adopted by the former military leaders which consisted in "apprehending suspects, keeping them secretly in captivity under inhuman conditions, subjecting them to torture in the aim of obtaining information so as ultimately to put them at the disposition of the courts or the National Executive Power or else to eliminate them physically." It also establishes the responsibility of those who carried out these men's orders directly and states that obedience to orders does not excuse those who carried out aberrant crimes.

1986:

The Supreme Court confirms the convictions, though it reduces Viola's and Agosti's sentences. The Federal Chamber hands down prison sentences to the former chiefs of police of Buenos Aires, Colonel Ramón Camps and General Pablo Ovidio Riccheri, and to their former assistant chief, Commissioner Miguel Osvaldo Etchecolatz, as well as to Dr. Jorge Bergés and Corporal Norberto Cozzani. The entire pyramid of repression is thus covered, from the highest-ranking military leaders to the low ranking policemen and civilian collaborators.

The same court takes over the trial for the events at the Navy School of Mechanics. Alarmed by the military repercussions of the convictions, Alfonsín persuades Congress to sanction a law known as Full Stop: the judges will have 60 days to bring charges against all those implicated in human rights violations. Once that time has elapsed, all such cases will be considered invalid.

1987:

In February, when the sixty-day statute of limitations ends, Federal Chambers throughout the country have not brought charges against thirty or forty members of the military, as the government had hoped, but against almost four hundred. In the ESMA proceedings, the Federal Chamber of the Capital orders the arrest of nineteen men, among them admirals, officers, and noncommissioned officers. As the summonses continue to reach officers facing charges in other parts of the country, the military tension grows.

On April 15, Lieutenant Colonel Ernesto Barreiro ignores a summons from the Federal Chamber of Córdoba to give testimony in response to charges of torture and treasonous homicide. Lieutenant Colonel Aldo Rico occupies the School of Infantry in the largest military garrison in Argentina. His commandos, known as the *carapintadas* because their faces are painted, demand that the trials of their comrades be brought to a halt. "The shifting terrain of the law and judicial chicanery is not the soldier's natural habitat. The soldier is trained to show his teeth and bite; combat is his proper environment and his power resides in holding a monopoly on violence," he explains in a document. The president orders the uprising to be repressed, but the military columns take several days to travel a few hundred kilometers. In front of the Legislative Assembly, Alfonsín declares that no civilian or member of the military can use force to negotiate his judicial situation and reaffirms the equality of all before the law. He announces to a crowd that has gathered in the Plaza de Mayo to condemn the uprising that he will go personally to the garrisons to demand the surrender of the *carapintadas*. Upon his return, he calls them "the heroes of the Malvinas war" and asks the demonstrators to disperse, stating that "the house is in order." He bids them good-bye with a disconcerting, "Happy Easter."

In July, he persuades Congress to approve the law of Due Obedience, which exempts from guilt those who tortured or murdered in fulfillment of orders. Only the former military leaders and a select group of generals and former leaders of army corps and security zones remain in prison. Among those set free are Astiz and Pernías.

1988:

The *carapintadas* take part in two new uprisings, the first led by Rico and the second by Colonel Mohamed Alí Seineldín, a former adviser to Panamanian strongman Manuel Noriega. Seineldín says he is receiving directives from the Virgin Mary.

1989:

In January, a remnant of the vanished People's Revolutionary Army occupies the military facility of La Tablada after denouncing a pact between the *carapintadas* and the Peronists which is intended to force Alfonsín to resign.

International credit organizations cut off Argentina's financing, which unleashes a run against the peso. In May, the Peronist candidate Carlos Menem is elected president. Hyperinflation devalues salaries and supermarkets are ransacked for food in several parts of the country. Alfonsín resigns from the presidency and Menem assumes it five months before his term officially begins. In October, he signs a pardon for four hundred officers and non-commissioned officers charged in the *carapintada* rebellions (among them Rico and Seineldín) and for the three former commanders in chief sentenced by the military courts for their role in the Malvinas war, as well as four dozen generals, admirals, colonels, and captains who remained in prison for human rights violations.

1990:

In December, Seineldín leads a new uprising, 48 hours before the arrival in Argentina of President George Bush; the rebellion is put down, weapon in hand, by the assistant chief of staff of the army, General Martín Balza. Menem wants to have the prisoners shot, but is dissuaded by his advisers. Days later, he pardons the former members of the military junta sentenced by the courts, as well as the Montonero leaders Mario Firmenich (sentenced to thirty years' imprisonment), Fernando Vaca Narvaja, and Roberto Perdía (who was living in exile).

1995:

Lieutenant Commander Adolfo Scilingo becomes the first member of the Argentine military to speak openly and at length about his participation in the dirty war.

Key Figures

Acosta, Jorge A. ("El Tigre"):
Chief of intelligence of the task force at the Navy School of Mechanics (ESMA) from 1976 to 1978, while Massera was commander in chief. The navy forced him to retire when a photograph of him with a showgirl who was wearing his officer's cap appeared in a magazine. Arrested on charges of illegal deprivation of liberty, torture, and homicide in February 1987, he was set free that same year under the Due Obedience law.

Agosti, Ramón:
A former brigadier general and commander in chief of the air force, he was part of the military junta that took control of the government on March 24, 1976. The civilian courts sentenced him to four and a half years' imprisonment. The Supreme Court reduced the sentence to three years and nine months, which he finished serving in June 1988. He is the only member of the military who served the entire sentence given him by the courts.

Alfonsín, Raúl:
President of Argentina, democratically elected in 1983 by the Radical Civic Union. He formed a commission to investigate the disappearances that took place during the military dictatorship and ordered that nine former

commanders in chief of the armed forces, among them three former de facto presidents, be brought to trial. In 1987, after the first *carapintada* uprising, he sent Congress the law of Due Obedience, which exempted the direct executors of the crimes committed during the dirty war from responsibility. Because of hyperinflation and the looting of supermarkets, he resigned from the presidency in May 1989, five months before completing his term of office.

Anchézar, Juan Carlos:
Retired vice admiral. He worked very closely with Massera and was the person who certified that Scilingo was not experiencing psychiatric difficulties. Menem appointed him undersecretary of State Intelligence.

Arduino, Adolfo:
As defense chief of the ESMA, he ordered Scilingo to go on his first flight. No charges were ever brought against him. In 1988 he became a vice admiral, and the following year he retired.

Arosa, Ramón:
Admiral, chief of staff of the navy under Alfonsín from 1983 to 1989. He was Scilingo's commanding officer at the Military House of the Presidency.

Astiz, Alfredo:
Commander. Was a member of the task force at ESMA. In 1987 he was arrested and charged with illegal deprivation of liberty and the torturing to death of political prisoners, among them two French nuns. He was set free by the law of Due Obedience, but the Chamber of Appeals in Paris sentenced him to life imprisonment in absentia, and therefore he cannot leave Argentina.

Balza, Martín Antonio:
General, chief of staff of the army from 1991 to the present. He was outside of Argentina during the first years of the military dictatorship and later he fought in the Malvinas (Falklands) war. In 1990, he repressed the last of the *carapintada* uprisings, weapon in hand. In 1995, and during the debate that followed the publication of this book, he acknowledged the atrocities that were committed by the army during the dirty war and offered a modern doctrine of obedience: a soldier must disobey immoral or illegal orders.

Barreiro, Ernesto Guillermo ("Nabo"):
Former lieutenant colonel. He was the chief torturer at the army concentration camp in Córdoba. On April 15, 1987, he ignored a summons from the

civilian courts that sought to question him on charges of torture and treasonous homicide and took refuge in a military facility. Thus began the Easter
Week uprising, which culminated in the law of Due Obedience, exempting
all officers below the rank of general from prosecution.

Bignone, Benito:
General. The last military dictator. He was appointed by his peers in
June 1982, after the disastrous Malvinas war, and handed over the presidency to Raúl Alfonsín in December 1983. Upon leaving office he was
arrested by the civilian authorities for the disappearance of two enlisted
soldiers from a military unit under his command. The military courts
left him at liberty during the trial, which ended with the law of Due
Obedience.

Bonafini, Hebe:
One of the leaders of the Mothers of the Plaza de Mayo, who have demonstrated in front of the Pink House (Argentina's White House) for their disappeared children every Thursday since April 1977. Two of her children
are among the disappeared.

Chamorro, Rubén Jacinto:
Admiral, director of ESMA. Under the aliases "Máximo" and "Delfín"
(Dolphin) he commanded the ESMA task force that operated after the
1976 coup. He was arrested and charged with illegal deprivation of liberty,
torture, and the murder of prisoners. He died in jail in 1986.

Daleo, Graciela:
A leader of the Peronist guerilla group, the Montoneros, who was abducted
in 1977. She was tortured at ESMA and set free in 1979. She was a witness
in the trial of the former military leaders and was the only person who did
not accept Menem's pardon in 1989, but the Supreme Court declared that
the pardon could not be rejected.

Devoto, Jorge:
Retired navy lieutenant junior grade. After going to his commander in chief
to ask about his father-in-law, who had been abducted, Devoto never reappeared. Scilingo heard rumors at ESMA that Devoto was thrown into the
sea while conscious.

Domon, Alice and Duquet, Leonie:
The two French nuns abducted in December 1977 by the task force based
at ESMA, where they were tortured and murdered.

Ferrer, Jorge Osvaldo:
Admiral, chief of staff of the navy between 1989 and 1993. As commander of the navy's only aircraft carrier, he was the commanding officer who helped Scilingo retire from the navy.

Firmenich, Mario Eduardo:
Chief of the Peronist guerrillas known as the Montoneros. Extradited from Brazil in 1984. In 1986 he was sentenced to thirty years' imprisonment for kidnapping the businessmen Juan and Jorge Born. Menem pardoned him in 1990.

Galtieri, Leopoldo:
Former general, one of the leaders of the repression in the provinces of Santa Fe, Entre Ríos, Corrientes, Chaco, Formosa, and Misiones. He took control of the government by force in December 1981. In April 1982, he ordered the occupation of the Malvinas, or Falkland Islands, and in June of that year he was thrown out of the presidency after the defeat by Great Britain. In 1986, the military courts sentenced him to fourteen years in prison for his role in the Malvinas war, and in 1988 the civil courts reduced the sentence to twelve years. He was also tried for human rights violations committed during the dirty war. Menem pardoned him in 1989.

Hagelin, Dagmar:
A seventeen-year-old girl of Swedish-Argentine extraction captured by the ESMA task force on January 27, 1977, during an operation in which Astiz wounded her in the back. She never reappeared. The Federal Chamber considered the case against Astiz to have been proven, but absolved him in December 1986 because the statute of limitations had expired.

Harguindeguy, Albano Eduardo:
Army general. Chief of police in 1975 and minister of the interior for the military government from 1976 to 1981. Tried for the extortionist kidnapping of two businessmen. Menem pardoned him in 1989.

Hesayne, Miguel Esteban:
Bishop of Viedma, in Patagonia. One of the few members of the Church hierarchy who condemned torture and stood up to the military government. Called for the Conference of Bishops to repent for not having done the same.

Ibáñez, Victor:
Noncommissioned army officer who was in charge of guarding the prisoners at the largest concentration camp in Buenos Aires. After Scilingo's

confession, he revealed that the army also threw prisoners into the sea. He identified half a dozen of the victims. The following day, Balza made a public admission of the facts.

Juppé, Alain:
In 1994, as France's minister of foreign relations, he met with the Mothers of the Plaza de Mayo in Buenos Aires and declared that his country would not forget the two nuns "tortured and murdered for their way of thinking." In 1995, as prime minister of France, he supported his ambassador's expressions of displeasure with the chief of the navy's praise for Commander Astiz's "moral condition." French ambassador Renaud Vignal called Astiz "a murderer." Because of that episode, the government forced Astiz to request retirement.

Laghi, Pio:
The papal nuncio to Argentina from 1974 to 1981. Played tennis with Massera and consulted with his successor, Armando Lambruschini. According to the wife of a disappeared man, to whom Laghi was of some assistance, Lambruschini asked the Vatican's representative what to do with a group of forty prisoners whom he didn't want to kill but who he was afraid would reveal what they had lived through. Previously, the navy had smuggled another group of prisoners out of the country with visas the military vicar's office had obtained thanks to Laghi's contact with the Venezuelan ambassador. The nuncio saved several lives, but never condemned what he knew was taking place.

Lambruschini, Armando:
Commander in chief of the navy and a member of the military junta between 1978 and 1981. In 1985, the civilian courts sentenced him to eight years' imprisonment for illegal deprivation of liberty and torture. In 1978, the Montoneros exploded a bomb inside his house and his fifteen-year-old daughter Paula was killed. Menem pardoned him in 1990.

López, Fausto:
Retired admiral, former director of personnel and third in command of the navy. When Scilingo wrote his initial letters demanding that the truth be told about the disappeared, López first offered him money to shut up, then threatened to strip him of his naval benefits. Menem made him second in command of internal security.

López Rega, José:
A police corporal and esoteric astrologer known as "El Brujo" ("The Sorcerer"), he became the butler at Perón's house in Madrid. Upon return-

ing to Argentina in 1973, he was appointed a minister and promoted to commissioner general of the police. Once in power, he organized the death squads known as the Triple A. Pressure from the military forced him to leave the government and the country in 1975. After a decade during which his whereabouts were a mystery, he was arrested in Miami, Florida, in 1986 and extradited to Argentina. He died in prison in 1989.

Maggio, Horacio Domingo:
A Montonero union leader. In 1978, he managed to escape from ESMA and revealed what was taking place there, but he was recaptured and killed by the task force.

Martínez de Perón, María Estela "Isabelita":
A cabaret dancer whom Juan D. Perón, thirty years her senior, met and married during his exile in Franco's Spain. In 1973, she was elected vice president and assumed the presidency on July 1, 1974, after Perón's death. During her brief and chaotic tenure in office, López Rega organized the death squads known as the Triple A. She was overthrown by the military on March 24, 1976.

Massera, Emilio Eduardo:
Commander in chief of the navy after 1975 and from 1976 to 1978 a member of the military junta that overthrew the government of Isabel Perón. Arrested in 1983 by the civilian courts for the murder of a mistress's husband. In 1985, the Federal Chamber of Buenos Aires sentenced him to life imprisonment. Menem pardoned him in 1990.

Massot, Vicente:
Vice minister of defense under President Menem. Recommended that Menem request the Senate to confirm the promotions of Rolón and Pernías. Resigned in January 1994 over the resulting scandal.

Mayorga, Horacio:
Admiral, was chief of naval aviation and Astiz's defender in the military courts. The first navy officer to acknowledge that torture was used on the prisoners at ESMA.

Mendía, Luis María:
Vice admiral, in 1976 was commander of naval operations and as such drew up the plans for the navy's participation in the dirty war. Announced to all the officers at the country's largest naval base that prisoners would be secretly executed and that the method of the flight had been approved by

the church hierarchy. He was tried in 1984 but set free because the statute of limitations had expired.

Menem, Carlos:
President of Argentina, democratically elected in 1989 by the Justicialista Party. After a constitutional reform, he was reelected in 1995. In 1990, he pardoned the former members of the military junta who had ordered his arrest in 1976.

Mignone, Emilio:
President of the Center for Legal and Social Studies, a human rights organization. His daughter Mónica was kidnapped in 1976 along with the nun Mónica Quinteiro and never reappeared. He filed a lawsuit that eventually persuaded the courts to declare a right to mourning and the burial of bodies, but the armed forces continued to deny that they had any information about his daughter.

Molina Pico, Enrique Emilio:
Admiral, appointed chief of staff of the navy by President Carlos Menem in 1993. Fought in the Malvinas war. His wife's sister was Mónica Quinteiro, the nun who was abducted, tortured, and killed by the ESMA task force in 1976.

Moreno Ocampo, Luis:
Former prosecutor who brought charges against Videla, Massera, Pernías, and Astiz. In 1991, Scilingo confessed his participation in the flights to Moreno Ocampo, who told him that the judicial process was closed and did not make the confession public.

Pernías, Antonio:
Naval commander whose promotion was rejected by the Senate in 1994. After the 1976 military coup, he was a member of the ESMA task force. In 1987, he was arrested and accused of torturing political prisoners to death, among them the two French nuns. He was set free by the law of Due Obedience.

Perón, Juan D.:
The central figure in twentieth-century Argentine politics. Army general and constitutional president between 1946 and 1955, when he was overthrown by a military coup. He returned after eighteen years in exile and was reelected in 1973. He died in office in July 1974.

Quinteiro, Mónica:
Catholic nun abducted in 1976 and seen by other prisoners at ESMA. She

never reappeared. Her sister is the wife of Menem's chief of staff of the navy, Admiral Molina Pico.

Quinteiro, Oscar:
Retired captain. Father of Mónica Quinteiro and father-in-law of Admiral Molina Pico. He interceded with Massera, who had once been his student, on his daughter's behalf. Massera told him his daughter was not being held by the navy.

Rico, Aldo:
Leader of the April 1987 *carapintada* rebellion demanding that President Alfonsín put an end to the trials of members of the military for their actions during the dirty war. Today he is the national representative of a small right-wing party aligned with the government.

Rolón, Juan Carlos:
Navy commander whose promotion was rejected by the Senate in 1994. After the 1976 military coup, he was a member of the ESMA task force.

Sábato, Ernesto:
Argentine novelist and painter. In 1984, presided over the National Commission on the Disappeared.

Solarz de Osatinsky, Sara:
Her husband, Montonero leader Marcos Osatinsky, and two teenage children were killed by the military. She was held prisoner at ESMA from May 14, 1977 to December 19, 1978. In 1979, together with her companions in captivity Ana María Martí and María Alicia Milia de Pirles, she presented lengthy testimony before the French National Assembly, in which she mentioned the flights that were used to kill the prisoners.

Timerman, Jacobo:
Owner and editor of the daily paper *La Opinión*. In April 1977, he was kidnapped by the military and his newspaper was seized. In 1979, the Supreme Court ordered that he be set free and the military junta deported him. During his testimony in the 1985 trial, he said that Massera and other navy officers justified the clandestine killings because "it would be very difficult to send people to the firing squad against the Pope's wishes."

Urien, Julio César:
Ensign who received instruction on torturing at ESMA in 1971. In November 1972, he tried to foment a revolt at ESMA in support of Perón's

return. He became a member of the Montoneros and was arrested in 1975. He remained a prisoner until the end of the dictatorship.

Vaca, Lieutenant:
A lawyer and cousin of Tigre Acosta who joined the ESMA task force under the pretext of being a member of the military. He participated in Scilingo's first flight, and Scilingo accuses him of having, for purely personal reasons, planned the kidnapping and murder of a woman lawyer who was not at all politically active.

Videla, Jorge Rafael:
Commander in chief of the army after 1975 and a member of the military junta that overthrew Isabel Perón's government. He was de facto president of the country until 1981. In 1985, the Federal Chamber of Buenos Aires sentenced him to life imprisonment and stripped him of the rank of general. Menem pardoned him in 1990.

Villar, Alberto:
Police commissioner, former chief of police, reviled as an organizer of the death squads known as the Triple A. Killed by the Montoneros in 1975. Twenty years later, Menem vindicated him as "one of the greatest leaders."

Viola, Roberto:
Successively chief of staff and commander in chief of the army after the 1976 coup. The military junta designated him to succeed Videla as president. During a visit to the United States as president-elect in 1990, he said that if the Nazis had won the war, the Nuremberg trials would have taken place in Richmond, Virginia. He became president in March 1991, but was overthrown in December by the man to whom he had yielded command of the army, Leopoldo Galtieri, who claimed he was acting for health reasons. Sentenced to seventeen years' imprisonment in 1985. The Supreme Court reduced the sentence to sixteen and a half years. Menem pardoned him in 1990, and he died in 1994.

Walsh, Rodolfo:
One of the greatest Argentine writers of the twentieth century, author of short stories, detective novels, investigative reports on the political violence, and plays. He was linked to the Montonero guerrillas but had disagreements with the group's national leadership, whose militarism he objected to. After the 1976 military coup, he organized the clandestine diffusion of information on the horrors of the dictatorship's concentration camps. On March 25, 1977, after he had disseminated by mail an "Open

Letter from a Writer to the Military Junta," which Gabriel García Márquez described as "a masterpiece of universal journalism," a squad from ESMA under Astiz's command tried to kidnap him. Walsh resisted and was riddled with bullets. A prisoner saw his body at ESMA, where it may have been incinerated.